BATTLIN

UNBELIE

# BATTLING UNBELIEF

## JOHN PIPER

Multnomah Publishers

BATTLING UNBELIEF
published by Multnomah Publishers
*A division of Random House, Inc.*

© 2007 by Desiring God Foundation
International Standard Book Number:1-59052-960-X

Cover design by The DesignWorks Group
Interior design by Katherine Lloyd, The DESK, Sisters, Oregon

*Italics* in Scripture quotations are the author's emphasis.
Unless otherwise indicated, Scripture quotations are from:
The Holy Bible, *English Standard Version.* © 2001 by Crossway Bibles,
a division of Good News Publishers.
Used by permission. All rights reserved.
Scripture quotations marked KJV are from the King James Version of the Bible.
Scripture references marked RSV are from *The Revised Standard Version.*
Copyright 1946, 1952, 1971, 1973 by the Division of Christian Education
of the National Council of the Churches of Christ in the U.S.A.
Scripture quotations marked NASB are from *The New American Standard Bible.*
© 1960, 1962, 1963, 1968, 1971, 1972, 1973, 1975, 1977, 1995 by the Lockman
Foundation. Used by permission.

*Multnomah* is a trademark of Multnomah Publishers,
and is registered in the U.S. Patent and Trademark Office.
The colophon is a trademark of Multnomah Publishers, Inc.
Printed in the United States of America

For information:
Multnomah Publishers
12265 Oracle Boulevard, Suite 200
Colorado Springs, CO 80921
Library of Congress Cataloging-in-Publication Data
Piper, John, 1946-
Battling unbelief / John Piper.
   p. cm.
Includes indexes.
ISBN 1-59052-960-X
1. Belief and doubt. 2. Faith. 3. Sin. I. Title.
BT774.P57 2007
248.8'6--dc22
                                            2006031790

07 08 09 10–10 9 8 7 6 5 4 3 2 1 0

To
Ruth Eulalia Piper
1918–1974
May her memory be honored
in the holiness of her heirs

# CONTENTS

# INTRODUCTION

In *To End All Wars*, Ernest Gordon tells the true story of a group of POW's working on the Burma Railway during World War II. The scene was made even more unforgettable because of the movie by the same title.

The day's work had ended; the tools were being counted, as usual. As the party was about to be dismissed, the Japanese guard shouted that a shovel was missing. He insisted that someone had stolen it to sell to the Thais. Striding up and down before the men, he ranted and denounced them for their wickedness, and most unforgivable of all their ingratitude to the Emperor. As he raved, he worked himself up into a paranoid fury. Screaming in broken English, he demanded that the guilty one step forward to take his punishment. No one moved; the guard's rage reached new heights of violence.

"All die! All die!" he shrieked.

To show that he meant what he said, he cocked

his rifle, put it to his shoulder and looked down the sights, ready to fire at the first man at the end of them.

At that moment the Argyll [Highlander] stepped forward, stood stiffly to attention, and said calmly, "I did it."

The guard unleashed all his whipped-up hate; he kicked the helpless prisoner and beat him with his fists. Still the Argyll stood rigidly to attention, with the blood streaming down his face. His silence goaded the guard to an excessive rage. Seizing his rifle by the barrel, he lifted it high over his head and with a final howl, brought it down on the skull of the Argyll, who sank limply to the ground and did not move. Although it was perfectly clear that he was dead, the guard continued to beat him and stopped only when exhausted.

The men of the work detail picked up their comrade's body, shouldered their tools and marched back to camp. When the tools were counted again at the guard-house no shovel was missing.[1]

The guard had miscounted. The young soldier who stepped forward had not stolen a shovel. He had given his life for his friends.

## WHAT JUST HAPPENED?
## MERE DEVOTION TO DUTY?

There is more than one way to commend this young man's sacrifice. One would be to say, "That's the kind of devotion to duty we need more of in this day of self-centeredness and cowardice." Another would be to say—this is the way I would say it—"That is the kind of love that *faith in future grace* releases. We need far more of that kind of love in this day of self-centeredness and cowardice."

These two ways of commending the sacrifice are not necessarily in conflict. But they might be. The first way speaks of a kind of "devotion to duty." The second speaks of the transforming power of faith in God's promises. In contrasting these two, we need to ask, What kind of duty was it? That is the crucial question. The external action does not tell the decisive story. What was going on in the heart—toward God and man? The Bible cautions us that people can sacrifice their lives, but not love people or God. "If I give away all I have, and *if I deliver up my body to be burned,* but have not love, I gain nothing" (1 Corinthians 13:3). When the apostle Paul says this, he means there is a kind of "devotion to duty" that God does not honor. It gains nothing.

That may seem strange, since Jesus himself said, "Greater love has no one than this, that someone lays down his life for his friends" (John 15:13). Yes, that is what great love does. It lays down its life. But whether that act is truly loving depends on what is going on in the heart, not just on the external action.

## THE FRUIT OF FAITH IN FUTURE GRACE

Another way to describe the young soldier's sacrifice is to say that faith in future grace welled up in his heart and gave him the love and courage to give his life for his friends. He may have thought in a flash: "Jesus, you died for me. My sins are forgiven. I have eternal life. I love you. You are my greatest treasure. I am eager to be with you. My friends are not all ready to die. I am. To live is Christ and to die is gain. Here I come." Perhaps he took fifteen seconds to remind himself of what Christ had done for him, and what that meant for his future after death. Then, sustained by his faith in God's promises, he stepped out and died. This is the fruit of faith in future grace.

The difference between the sacrifice that comes from sheer devotion to duty and the sacrifice that comes from faith in God's future grace is that the first highlights my strong resolve, and the second highlights the glory of God's grace. The aim of this book is to magnify the value of Christ by feeding faith in future grace and helping Christians battle the opposite, namely, unbelief in God's promises that leads to Christ-dishonoring sin.

## WHERE THE BOOK CAME FROM

The eight chapters that follow are taken from a much larger book titled *The Purifying Power of Living by Faith in Future Grace*.[2] These are the application chapters—the ones that actually illustrate how faith in future grace severs the root of sin and sets free the stream of love. Our focus is on the very practical challenge of how to free ourselves from anxiety, pride, misplaced shame, impatience, covetousness, bitterness, despondency, and lust. My conviction is that unbelief in the promises of God (that is, future grace) is the root that sustains the life of these sins. Hence the title: *Battling Unbelief*.

It is a risk to publish these eight chapters without the

twenty-three chapters that surround them and explain the foundations and implications found in *Future Grace*. But I think it is worth the risk. Many people move from application back to foundation rather than the reverse. So I am hopeful that discovering in this smaller book some of the way faith works to liberate us from sin will send many readers to the larger work for a deeper biblical understanding.

## WE BATTLE FOR FAITH IN FUTURE GRACE

"Battling unbelief," is another way of saying, "Living by faith in future grace." The "unbelief" that I have in mind is the failure to trust the promises of God that sustain our radical obedience in the future. These promises refer to what God plans to do for us in the future, and that is what I mean by future grace. It is *grace*, because it is good for us and totally undeserved. And it is *future* in that it hasn't happened to us yet but may in the next five seconds or the next five thousand years.

For the Christian the promises of God are spectacular. They relate to our immediate future, before this minute is over, and our eternal future.

- "My God will supply every need of yours according to his riches in glory in Christ Jesus." (Philippians 4:19)

- "Surely goodness and mercy shall follow me all the days of my life." (Psalm 23:6)

- "No good thing does he withhold from those who walk uprightly." (Psalm 84:11)

- "It is your Father's good pleasure to give you the kingdom." (Luke 12:32)

- "I am your God; I will strengthen you, I will help you, I will uphold you with my righteous right hand." (Isaiah 41:10)

- "All things are yours...the world or life or death or the present or the future—all are yours, and you are Christ's, and Christ is God's." (1 Corinthians 3:21–23)

- "For those who love God all things work together for good, for those who are called according to his purpose." (Romans 8:28)

- "I am with you always, to the end of the age." (Matthew 28:20)

- "Neither death nor life...nor anything else in all creation, will be able to separate us from the love of God in Christ Jesus our Lord." (Romans 8:38–39)

These, and hundreds more, are there in the Bible to sustain our faith in God's future grace. The ultimate gift at the end of them all is God himself. Christ died not mainly to make things go well for us, but to bring us to God. "Christ also suffered once for sins, the righteous for the unrighteous, *that he might bring us to God*" (1 Peter 3:18). "Whom have I in heaven but *you*? And there is nothing on earth that I desire besides *you*" (Psalm 73:25). "I say to the LORD, 'You are my

Lord; I have no good apart from you'" (Psalm 16:2). "I count everything as loss because of the surpassing worth of knowing *Christ Jesus my Lord*" (Philippians 3:8). Jesus prays, "Father, I desire that they also, whom you have given me, may be with me where I am, *to see my glory*" (John 17:24). The final, best, highest, most satisfying gift of future grace is seeing and savoring God himself.[3]

## LEARNING TO FIGHT FIRE WITH FIRE

Being satisfied with all that God promises to be for us in Jesus Christ is the essence of faith in future grace. Keep in mind that when I speak of faith in future grace or satisfaction in what God promises to be for us, I am assuming that an essential part of that faith and that satisfaction is an embrace of Christ as our sin-bearing substitute whose perfect obedience to God is imputed to us through faith. In other words, faith in future grace embraces the *ground* of all the promises as well as the promises themselves. It treasures Christ as the one whose blood and righteousness provides the foundation for all future grace. *And* it treasures all that God now promises to be for us in Christ because of that foundational work. Whenever I speak of faith as being satisfied with all God is for us in Jesus, I am including all of this in that faith.

This faith is the power that severs the root of sin. Sin has power because of the promises it makes to us. It talks like this: "If you lie on your tax returns, you will have extra money to get what will make you happier." "If you look at this pornography you will have a surge of pleasure that is better than the joys of a clear conscience." "If you eat these cookies when no one is watching, it will soften your sense of woundedness and help you cope better than anything else just now." No one sins out of duty. We sin because we believe the deceitful promises that sin makes. The Bible warns "that none of you may be hardened by the *deceitfulness* of sin" (Hebrews 3:13). The promises of sin are lies.

Battling unbelief and fighting for faith in future grace means that we fight fire with fire. We throw against the promises of sin the promises of God. We take hold of some great promise God made about our future and say to a particular sin, "Match that!" In this way we do what Paul says in Romans 8:13, "By the Spirit...put to death the deeds of the body." John Owen wrote a book on that verse and summed it up with, "Be killing sin, or it will be killing you."[4] We kill sinful deeds before they happen by cutting the root of their life: the lies of sin.

Doing this "by the Spirit" means that we trust in the power of the Spirit and then wield the "sword of the Spirit," which is the word of God (Ephesians 6:17). The "word of God" is at its core the gospel, and then all that God has spoken in his revealed word. The gospel of Christ's death and resurrection is not only the core but the foundation of all the promises of God. That is the point of the logic of Romans 8:32, "He who did not spare his own Son but gave him up for us all, how will he not also with him graciously give us all things?" "All things" that we need—the fulfillment of all God's promises—are guaranteed by the Father's not sparing his Son. Or to put it positively, all the promises of God are secured for us because God sent his Son to live and die to cancel our sins and become our righteousness. So when I say that we wield the Word of God, the sword of the Spirit, what I mean is that we hold fast to this Christ-centered gospel truth with all its promises, and bank on them in every situation. We sever the lifeline of sin by the power of a superior promise. Or to put it more positively, we release the stream of love by faith in future grace. We become loving people by trusting in the promises of God.

## Jesus Loved Like This

The Bible says that Jesus endured the cross "for the joy that was set before him" (Hebrews 12:2). In other words, the greatest act of loving sacrifice that was ever performed was sustained by the confidence that God would bring Jesus through it into everlasting joy with a redeemed and worshiping people. That is the way our love is sustained as well.

But there is a difference. Our willingness to endure the sacrifices of love "for the joy that is set before us" was purchased by Jesus' willingness to do the same. His suffering covers our sins and sets us free to love. Our suffering in the path of love is based on his. His future joy came to him as his *right*. Ours comes to us as blood-bought *grace*. His suffering is not just a model. It is the ground of our hope. We are saved from sin and judgment by his suffering. Nevertheless, both his and ours are endured "for the joy that is set before us." His joy was a future right. Ours is future grace.

Therefore, without the death and resurrection of Jesus— that is, without *past* grace—we could expect no future grace. God's future grace toward us was purchased and guaranteed by his past grace toward us in Jesus' death and resurrection. As we have seen, Paul says this in one of the greatest verses in the Bible. "He who did not spare his own Son but gave him up for us all (past grace), how will he not also with him graciously give us all things (future grace)?" (Romans 8:32). Notice the glorious logic of heaven: *Because* God spared his Son no pain in saving us, *therefore* he will spare no omnipotent effort to give us all that we need forever. Absolutely certain future grace will come to those who trust Christ, because God infallibly secured it in not sparing his Son.

## WE BATTLE AS VICTORS

The very next verses say, "Who shall bring any charge against God's elect? It is God who justifies. Who is to condemn? Christ Jesus is the one who died—more than that, who was raised—who is at the right hand of God, who indeed is interceding for us" (Romans 8:33–34). This means that because of Christ, God has justified us. Past tense. We are now already counted righteous in Christ. No one can bring a successful charge against us. Christ died for us and lives for us. Thus, we battle unbelief and sin as those who in Christ already have the decisive victory. We already have our standing in heaven by faith in Christ. Christ is our righteousness. Christ is our perfection. We pursue holiness, not because we are not yet accepted by God, but because we are. This is the way Paul put it: "I press on to make it my own, because Christ Jesus has made me his own" (Philippians 3:12).

So I invite you to engage with me in the battle against

unbelief in the promises of God. I invite you to fight the fight of faith in future grace. And I invite you to rejoice that we can fight this fight not as though it doesn't matter, but knowing that it matters infinitely, and that God is with us to the end: "Be not dismayed, for I am your God; I will strengthen you, I will help you, I will uphold you with my righteous right hand" (Isaiah 41:10).

*When I am afraid,*
*I put my trust in you.*

PSALM 56:3

*Cast all your anxieties on him,*
*because he cares for you.*

1 PETER 5:7

*Therefore do not be anxious, saying,*
*"What shall we eat?" or*
*"What shall we drink?" or*
*"With what shall we wear?"*
*For the Gentiles seek after all these things,*
*and your heavenly Father knows that you need them all.*

MATTHEW 6:31–32

*Chapter One*

---

# BATTLING
# ANXIETY

## A PERSONAL TRIUMPH
## THROUGH FUTURE GRACE

When I was in junior and senior high school, I could not speak in front of a group. I became so nervous that my voice would completely choke up. It was not the common butterflies that most people deal with. It was a horrible and humiliating disability. It brought immense anxiety into my life. I could not give oral book reports in school. I couldn't run for any class offices at school, because I would have had to make campaign speeches. I could only give very short—several word—answers to the questions teachers would ask in class. In algebra class I was ashamed of how my hands shook when doing a problem on the blackboard. I couldn't lead out on the Sundays when our church gave the service over to the youth.

There were many tears. My mother struggled with me through it all, supporting me and encouraging me. We were sustained by God's grace, even though the "thorn" in my flesh was not removed. I managed to make it to college without any significant public speaking. But the battle with anxiety was intense. I knew that my life would be incredibly limited if there were no breakthrough. And I suspected that I would not be able to get through college without public speaking. In fact, Wheaton College required a speech class in those days. It loomed in front of me like a horrible concrete barricade.

In all these years, the grace of God had driven me deeper into God in desperation, rather than driving me away from God in anger. I thank God for that, with all my heart. Out of that maturing relationship came the sense that there just had to be a breakthrough.

One crucial opportunity came in Spanish class my fresh-man year. All of us had to give a short speech in Spanish in front of the rest of the class. There was no way around it. I felt like this was a make-or-break situation. Even as I write about it now, I don't laugh. I memorized the speech cold. I thought that memorizing would mean that I wouldn't have to look down at notes, and possibly lose my place, and have one of those horrible, paralyzing pauses. I also arranged to speak from behind a large tree-stump lectern that I could hold onto so that my shaking might be better controlled. But the main thing I did was cry out to God and lay hold on his promises of future grace. Even now the tears come to my eyes as I recall walking back and forth on Wheaton's front campus, pleading with God for a breakthrough in my life.

I don't remember those three moments of Spanish very clearly. I only remember that I made it through. Everyone knew I was nervous. There was that terrible silence that falls when people feel bad for you and don't know how to respond. But they didn't snicker, as so many kids had done in previous years. And the teacher was kind with his comments. But the overwhelming thing was that I got through it. Later I poured out my thanks to God in the autumn sunshine. Even now I feel deep gratitude for the grace God gave me that day.

Perhaps the most decisive event of the breakthrough came over a year later. I was staying at college for summer school. Chaplain Evan Welch invited me to pray in the summer school chapel. Several hundred students and faculty would be present. My first reaction was immediate rejection of the idea. But before I could turn it down, something stopped me. I found myself asking, "How long does the prayer have to be?" He said it didn't matter. It should just be from my heart.

Now this I had never even tried—to speak to God in front of hundreds of people. I amazed myself by saying I would do it. This prayer, I believe, proved to be a decisive turning point in my life. For the first time, I made a vow to God. I said, "Lord, if you will bring me through this without letting my voice break, I will never again turn down a speaking opportunity for you out of anxiety." That was 1966. The Lord answered with precious grace again, and to my knowledge, I have kept my vow.

There is more to the story as one future grace has been lavished on another. I do not presume to understand fully all the purposes of God in his timing. I would not want to relive my high-school years. The anxiety, the humiliation and shame, were so common, as to cast a pall over all those years. Hundreds of prayers went up, and what came down was not what I wanted at the time—the grace to endure. My interpretation now, thirty years later, is that God was keeping me back from excessive vanity and worldliness. He was causing me to ponder weighty things in solitude, while many others were breezily slipping into superficial patterns of life.

The Bible my parents gave me when I was fifteen is beside me right now on the table. It is well-marked. The assurance of Matthew 6:32 is underlined in red: "Your heavenly father knoweth that ye have need of all these things" (KJV). Already in those early teen years I was struggling to live by faith in future grace. The victories were modest, it seems. But, oh, how faithful and kind God has been.

## THE ASSOCIATES OF ANXIETY

In the decades that have followed I have learned much more about the fight against anxiety. I have learned, for instance, that anxiety is a condition of the heart that gives rise to many other sinful states of mind. Think for a moment how many different sinful actions and attitudes come from anxiety. Anxiety about finances can give rise to coveting and greed and hoarding and stealing. Anxiety about succeeding at some task can make you irritable and abrupt and surly. Anxiety about relationships can make you withdrawn and indifferent and uncaring about other people. Anxiety about how someone will respond to you can make you cover over the truth and lie about things. So if anxiety could be conquered, a mortal blow would be struck to many other sins.

## The Root of Anxiety

I have also learned something about the *root* of anxiety and the ax that can sever it. One of the most important texts has been the one I underlined when I was fifteen—the whole section of Matthew 6:25–34. Four times in this passage Jesus says that his disciples should not be anxious. Verse 25: "Do not be anxious about your life." Verse 27: "Which of you by being anxious can add a single hour to his span of life?" Verse 31: "Do not be anxious, saying, 'What shall we eat?'" Verse 34: "Do not be anxious about tomorrow."

Anxiety is clearly the theme of this text. It makes the root of anxiety explicit in verse 30: "But if God so clothes the grass of the field, which today is alive and tomorrow is thrown into the oven, will he not much more clothe you, O you of little *faith*?" In other words, Jesus says that the root of anxiety is inadequate faith in our Father's future grace. As unbelief gets the upper hand in our hearts, one of the effects is anxiety. The root cause of anxiety is a failure to trust all that God has promised to be for us in Jesus.

I can think of two kinds of disturbed responses to this truth. Let me tell you what they are and then give a biblical response to each of them before we look more closely at the battle against the unbelief of anxiety.

## Is This Good News?

One response would go like this: "This is not good news! In fact, it is very discouraging to learn that what I thought was a mere struggle with an anxious disposition is rather a far deeper struggle with whether I trust God." My response to this is to agree, but then to disagree. Suppose you had been having pain in your stomach and had been struggling with medicines and diets of all kinds to no avail. And then suppose that your doctor tells you, after a routine visit, that you have cancer in your small intestine. Would that be good news? You say: Emphatically not! And I agree.

But let me ask the question another way: Are you glad the doctor discovered the cancer while it is still treatable, and that indeed it can be very successfully treated? You say, yes, I am very glad that the doctor found the real problem. Again I agree. So finding out that you have cancer is not good news. It's bad news. But, in another sense, it is good to find out, because knowing what is really wrong is good, especially when your problem can be treated successfully.

That's what it's like to learn that the real problem behind anxiety is unbelief in the promises of God's future grace. In a sense, it's not good news, because the unbelief is a very serious cancer. But in another sense it is good news because knowing what is really wrong is good, especially because unbelief can be treated so successfully by our Great Physician. He is able to work in wonderfully healing ways when we cry out, "I believe; help my unbelief!" (Mark 9:24).

So I want to stress that finding out the connection between our anxiety and our unbelief is, in fact, very good news, because it is the only way to focus our fight on the real cause of our sin and get the victory that God can give us by the therapy of his Word and his Spirit. When Paul said, "Fight the *good* fight of faith," (1 Timothy 6:12), he called it *good* because the fight is focused on exactly the right cancer: unbelief.

## How Can I Have
## Any Assurance at All?

There is another possible response to the truth that our anxiety is rooted in our failure to live by faith in future grace. It goes like this: "I have to deal with feelings of anxiety almost every day; and so I feel like my faith in God's grace must be totally inadequate. So I wonder if I can have any assurance of being saved at all."

My response to this concern is a little different. Suppose you are in a car race and your enemy, who doesn't want you to finish the race, throws mud on your windshield. The fact that you temporarily lose sight of your goal, and start to swerve, does not mean that you are going to quit the race. And it certainly doesn't mean that you are on the wrong race track. Otherwise the enemy wouldn't bother you at all. What it means is that you should turn on your windshield wipers and use your windshield washer.

When anxiety strikes and blurs our vision of God's glory and the greatness of the future that he plans for us, this does not mean that we are faithless, or that we will not make it to heaven. It means our faith is being attacked. At first blow, our belief in God's promises may sputter and swerve. But whether we stay on track and make it to the finish line depends on whether, by grace, we set in motion a process of resistance—whether we fight back against the unbelief of anxiety. Will we turn on the windshield wipers and will we use our windshield washer?

Psalm 56:3 says, "When I am afraid, I put my trust in you." Notice it does not say, "I never struggle with fear." Fear strikes, and the battle begins. So the Bible does not assume that true believers will have no anxieties. Instead, the Bible tells us how to fight when they strike. For example, 1 Peter 5:7 says, "[Cast] all your anxieties on him, because he cares for you." It does *not* say, You will never feel any anxieties. It says, When you have them, cast them on God. When the mud splatters your windshield and you temporarily lose sight of the road and start to swerve in anxiety, turn on your wipers and squirt your windshield washer fluid.

So my response to the person who has to deal with feelings of anxiety every day is to say, That's more or less normal. At least it is for me, ever since my teenage years. The issue is, how do we fight them?

## THE TWO GREAT FAITH BUILDERS

The answer to that question is: We fight anxieties by fighting *against* unbelief and fighting *for* faith in future grace. And the way you fight this "good fight" is by meditating on God's assurances of future grace and by asking for the help of his Spirit. The windshield wipers are the promises of God that clear away the mud of unbelief, and the windshield washer fluid is the help of the Holy Spirit. The battle to be freed from sin is "by the *Spirit*" (Romans 15:16; 2 Thessalonians 2:13; 1 Peter 1:2) and by "the truth" (John 17:17, 19). The work of the Spirit and the Word of truth—especially the foundational truth of the gospel that guarantees all the promises of God. These are the great faith builders.

Without the softening work of the Holy Spirit, the wipers of the Word just scrape over the blinding clumps of unbelief.

Both are necessary—the Spirit and the Word. We read the promises of God and we pray for the help of his Spirit. And as the windshield clears so that we can see the welfare that God plans for us (Jeremiah 29:11), our faith grows stronger and the swerving of anxiety smoothes out.

## Seven Promises of Future Grace Against Anxiety

How does this actually work in practice? Here in Matthew 6 we have the example of anxiety about food and clothing. Even in America, with its extensive welfare system, anxiety over finances and housing can be intense. But Jesus says in verse 30 that this stems from inadequate faith in our Father's promise of future grace: "O you of *little faith*." And so this paragraph has at least seven promises designed by Jesus to help us fight the good fight against unbelief and be free from anxiety.

### Promise #1

> Therefore I tell you, do not be anxious about your life, what you will eat or what you will drink, nor about your body, what you will put on. Is not life more than food, and the body more than clothing? (Matthew 6:25)

This is an argument from the greater to the lesser. If God does the greater, then doing the lesser is all the more sure. In this verse, the greater thing is that God has given us life and bodies. These are vastly more complex and difficult to maintain than the mere provision of clothing. Yet God has done it. Therefore, how much more easily can God provide us with food and clothing. Moreover, no matter what happens, God will raise your body someday and preserve your life for his eternal fellowship.

## Promise #2

Look at the birds of the air: they neither sow nor reap nor gather into barns, and yet your heavenly Father feeds them. Are you not of more value than they? (Matthew 6:26)

If God is willing and able to feed such insignificant creatures as birds who cannot do anything to bring their food into being—as you can by farming—then he will certainly provide what you need, because you are worth a lot more than birds.

## Promise #3

And which of you by being anxious can add a single hour to his span of life? And why are you anxious about clothing? (Matthew 6:27–28)

This is a promise of sorts—the simple promise of reality: Anxiety will not do you any good. It's not the main argument, but sometimes we just have to get tough with ourselves and say, "Soul, this fretting is absolutely useless. You are not only messing up your own day, but a lot of other people's as well. Leave it with God and get on with your work." Anxiety accomplishes nothing worthwhile.

BATTLING ANXIETY ——————— 31

## Promise #4

> Consider the lilies of the field, how they grow: they
> neither toil nor spin, yet I tell you, even Solomon in
> all his glory was not arrayed like one of these. But if
> God so clothes the grass of the field, which today is
> alive and tomorrow is thrown into the oven, will he
> not much more clothe you, O you of little faith?
> (Matthew 6:28–30)

Compared to the flowers of the field you are a much
higher priority for God, because you will live forever, and can
thus bring him eternal praise. Nevertheless, God has such an
overflow of creative energy and care, he lavishes it on flowers
that last only a matter of days. So he will certainly take that
same energy and creative skill and use it to care for his children
who will live forever.

## Promise #5

> Therefore do not be anxious, saying, 'What shall we
> eat?' or 'What shall we drink?' or 'What shall we
> wear?' For the Gentiles seek after all these things, and
> your heavenly Father knows that you need them all.
> (Matthew 6:31–32)

Do not think that God is ignorant of your needs. He
knows all of them. And he is your "heavenly Father." He does
not look on indifferently, from a distance. He cares. He will
act to supply your need when the time is best.

## Promise #6

> But seek first the kingdom of God and his righteous-
> ness, and all these things will be added to you.
> (Matthew 6:33)

If you will give yourself to his cause in the world, rather than fretting about your private material needs, he will make sure that you have all you need to do his will and give him glory. This is similar to the promise of Romans 8:32, "Will [God] not also with [Christ] freely give us all things?"[5]

## Promise #7

> Therefore do not be anxious about tomorrow, for
> tomorrow will be anxious for itself. Sufficient for the
> day is its own trouble. (Matthew 6:34)

God will see to it that you are not tested in any given day more than you can bear (1 Corinthians 10:13). He will work for you, so that "as your days, so shall your strength be" (Deuteronomy 33:25). Every day will have no more trouble than you can bear; and every day will have mercies sufficient for that day's stress (Lamentations 3:22–23).

### "MY GOD WILL SUPPLY ALL YOUR NEEDS"

Paul learned these lessons from Jesus and applied them to the battle against anxiety in the church at Philippi. In Philippians 4:6 he said, "Do not be anxious about anything, but in everything by prayer and supplication with thanksgiving let your requests be made known to God." And then in verse 19 he gives the liberating promise of future grace, just as Jesus did: "My God will supply every need of yours according to his riches in glory in Christ Jesus." If we live by faith in this promise of future grace, it will be very hard for anxiety to survive. God's "riches in glory" are inexhaustible. He really means for us not to worry about our future.

## WHEN I AM ANXIOUS

We should follow the pattern of Jesus and Paul. We should battle the unbelief of anxiety with the promises of future grace. When I am anxious about some risky new venture or meeting, I battle unbelief with one of my most often-used promises, Isaiah 41:10. The day I left for three years in Germany my father called me long distance and gave me this promise on the telephone. For three years I must have quoted it to myself five hundred times to get me through periods of tremendous stress. "Fear not, for I am with you; be not dismayed, for I am your God; I will strengthen you, I will help you, I will uphold you with my righteous right hand." (Isaiah 41:10). When the motor of my mind is in neutral, the hum of the gears is the sound of Isaiah 41:10.

When I am anxious about my ministry being useless and empty, I fight unbelief with the promise of Isaiah 55:11. "So shall my word be that goes out from my mouth; it shall not return to me empty, but it shall accomplish that which I purpose, and shall succeed in the thing for which I sent it."

When I am anxious about being too weak to do my

work, I battle unbelief with the promise of Christ, "My grace is sufficient for you, for my power is made perfect in weakness" (2 Corinthians 12:9).

When I am anxious about decisions I have to make about the future, I battle unbelief with the promise, "I will instruct you and teach you in the way you should go; I will counsel you with my eye upon you" (Psalm 32:8).

When I am anxious about facing opponents, I battle unbelief with the promise, "If God is for us, who can be against us?" (Romans 8:31).

When I am anxious about the welfare of those I love, I battle unbelief with the promise that if I, being evil, know how to give good things to my children, how much more will "your Father who is in heaven give good things to those who ask him!" (Matthew 7:11). And I fight to maintain my spiritual equilibrium with the reminder that everyone who has left house or brothers or sisters or mother or father or children or lands, for Christ's sake will "receive a hundredfold now in this time, houses and brothers and sisters and mothers and children and lands, with persecutions, and in the age to come eternal life" (Mark 10:29–30).

When I am anxious about being sick, I battle unbelief with the promise, "Many are the afflictions of the righteous, but the LORD delivers him out of them all" (Psalm 34:19). And I take the promise with trembling: "Suffering produces endurance, and endurance produces character, and character produces hope, and hope does not put us to shame, because God's love has been poured into our hearts through the Holy Spirit who has been given to us" (Romans 5:3–5).

When I am anxious about getting old, I battle unbelief

with the promise, "Even to your old age I am he, and to gray hairs I will carry you. I have made, and I will bear; I will carry and will save" (Isaiah 46:4).

When I am anxious about dying, I battle unbelief with the promise that "none of us lives to himself, and none of us dies to himself. If we live, we live to the Lord, and if we die, we die to the Lord. So then, whether we live or whether we die, we are the Lord's. For to this end Christ died and lived again, that he might be Lord both of the dead and of the living" (Romans 14:7–9).

When I am anxious that I may make shipwreck of my faith and fall away from God, I battle unbelief with the promises, "He who began a good work in you will bring it to completion at the day of Jesus Christ" (Philippians 1:6); and, "He is able to save to the uttermost those who draw near to God through him, since he always lives to make intercession for them" (Hebrews 7:25).

This is the way of life that I am still learning as I enter my seventh decade. I write this book in the hope, and with the prayer, that you will join me. Let us make war, not with other people, but with our own unbelief. It is the root of anxiety, which, in turn, is the root of so many other sins. So let us turn on our windshield wipers and use the washer fluid, and keep our eyes fixed on the precious and very great promises of God. Take up the Bible, ask the Holy Spirit for help, lay the promises up in your heart, and fight the good fight—to *live by faith in future grace*.

Thus says the LORD:
"Let not the wise man boast in his wisdom,
let not the mighty man boast in his might,
let not the rich man boast in his riches,
but let him who boasts boast in this,
that he understands and knows me,
that I am the LORD who practices
steadfast love, justice, and righteousness in the earth.
For in these things I delight, declares the LORD."

JEREMIAH 9:23–24

The pleasure of pride is like the pleasure of scratching.
If there is an itch one does want to scratch;
but it is much nicer to have neither the itch
nor the scratch.
As long as we have the itch of self-regard
we shall want the pleasure of self-approval;
but the happiest moments are those when we forget our
precious selves and have neither but have everything else
(God, our fellow humans, animals,
the garden and the sky) instead.

C.S. LEWIS

Humble yourselves... under the mighty hand of God
so that at the proper time he may exalt you.

1 PETER 5:6

# Chapter Two

# BATTLING PRIDE

## THE SHADOW OF GOD

**H**umility is not a popular human trait in the modern world. It's not touted in the talk shows or celebrated in valedictory speeches or commended in diversity seminars or listed with corporate core values. And if you go to the massive self-help section of your sprawling mall bookstore, you won't find many titles celebrating humility.

The basic reason for this is not hard to find: Humility can only survive in the presence of God. When God goes, humility goes. In fact, you might say that humility follows God like a shadow. We can expect to find humility applauded in our society about as often as we find God applauded.

In my local newspaper, a guest editorial captured the atmosphere of our time that asphyxiates humility:

> There are some who naively cling to the nostalgic memory of God. The average churchgoer takes a few

hours out of the week to experience the sacred....
But the rest of the time, he is immersed in a society
that no longer acknowledges God as an omniscient
and omnipotent force to be loved and worshiped....
Today we are too sophisticated for God. We can stand
on our own; we are prepared and ready to choose and
define our own existence.[6]

In this atmosphere, humility cannot survive. It disappears with God. When God is neglected, the runner-up god takes his place, namely, man. And that, by definition, is the opposite of humility, namely, the haughty spirit called pride. So the atmosphere we breathe is hostile to humility.

## AN APPETITE FOR GOD IN THE HEART

The point of this chapter is that a haughty spirit is a form of unbelief and that the way to battle the unbelief of pride is by faith in future grace. Trusting God and being arrogant are opposites: "An *arrogant* man stirs up strife, but he who trusts in the LORD will prosper" (Proverbs 28:25, NASB). That's why Stephen Charnock said, "A proud faith is as much a contradiction as a humble devil."[7] To see why faith and pride are opposites we need to remind ourselves what faith is.

I have argued more fully in *Future Grace* that the heart of biblical faith in Jesus is coming to him for the satisfaction of all that God is for us in him.[8] Jesus said in John 6:35, "I am the bread of life; whoever *comes* to me shall not hunger, and whoever *believes* in me shall never thirst." From this we may draw out the truth that *belief* in Jesus means coming to Jesus for the satisfaction of all that God is for us in him. And *unbelief* is a turning away from Jesus in order to seek satisfaction in other things.

*Belief* is not merely an *agreement* with facts in the head; it is also an *appetite* for God in the heart, which fastens on Jesus for satisfaction. "Whoever comes to me shall not hunger, and whoever believes in me shall never thirst!" Therefore, eternal life is not given to people who merely *think* that Jesus is the Son of God. It is given to people who *drink* from Jesus as the Son of God. "The water that I will give him will become in him a spring of water welling up to eternal life" (John 4:14). He is also the bread of life, and those who *feed* on him for nourishment and satisfaction live by him. "I am the living bread that came down from heaven. If anyone *eats* of this bread, he will live forever" (John 6:51). The point of these images of *drinking* and *eating* is to make clear the essence of faith. It is more than believing that there is such a thing as water and food; and it is more than believing that Jesus is life-giving water and food. Faith is coming to Jesus and *drinking* the water and *eating* the food so that we find our hearts satisfied in him.

## TURNING FROM SATISFACTION IN GOD TO SATISFACTION IN SELF

With this background we will see more clearly that pride is a species of unbelief. *Unbelief* is a turning away from God and his Son in order to seek satisfaction in other things.

*Pride* is a turning away from God specifically to take satisfaction in *self*. So pride is one specific form of unbelief. And its antidote is the wakening and strengthening of faith in future grace.

In chapter 5, we will see that *covetousness* is turning away from God, usually to find satisfaction in things. In chapter 8, we will see that *lust* is turning away from God to find satisfaction in sex. We will see that *bitterness* is turning away from God to find satisfaction in revenge (chapter 6). *Impatience* is turning away from God to find satisfaction in your own uninterrupted plan of action (chapter 4). *Anxiety*, *misplaced shame*, and *despondency* are various conditions of the heart when these efforts of unbelief miscarry (chapters 1, 3, and 7).

But deeper than all these forms of unbelief is the unbelief of pride, because self-determination and self-exaltation lie behind all these other sinful dispositions. Every turning from God—for anything—presumes a kind of autonomy or independence that is the essence of pride. Turning from God assumes that one knows better than God. Thus pride lies at the root of every turning from God. It is the root of every act of distrust toward God. Or, more accurately, pride is not so much the *root* as it is the *essence* of unbelief, and its remedy is faith in future grace. Thus the battle against pride is the battle against unbelief; and the fight for humility is the fight of faith in future grace.

Biblical references to pride can be categorized as different ways of distrusting God. Each text on pride reveals what we refuse to trust God for. Or, more specifically, each one shows what we prefer to find in ourselves.

## God's Great Competitors

In Jeremiah 9:23 God says, "Let not the wise man boast in his *wisdom*, let not the mighty man boast in his *might*, let not the rich man boast in his *riches*." In those three phrases, God names his great competitors for the boast of the human heart. Each one—wisdom, might, and riches—tempts us to take satisfaction in ourselves—our intelligence, our strength, our material resources. Each one lures us away from trusting God as the superior satisfaction above them all. It is radically humbling to confess that the source of all our joy resides outside ourselves.

## When Knowledge Puffs Up

Take wisdom and intelligence, for example. The apostle Paul warns that "'knowledge' puffs up, but love builds up" (1 Corinthians 8:1). This does not mean he favors ignorance and irrationality: "Do not be children in your *thinking*. Be infants in evil, but in your *thinking* be mature" (1 Corinthians 14:20). G. K. Chesterton, the British Catholic journalist-author who died in 1936, warned that in the twentieth century we are not clear about the relationship between intellectual conviction and pride.

> What we suffer from... is humility in the wrong place. Modesty has moved from the organ of ambition. Modesty has settled upon the organ of conviction; where it was never meant to be. A man was meant to be doubtful about himself, but undoubting about the truth; this has been exactly reversed. Nowadays the

part of a man that a man does assert is exactly the part he ought not to assert—himself. The part he doubts is exactly the part he ought not to doubt—the Divine Reason.[9]

Paul is not calling into question the necessity of firm conviction and true knowledge. Nevertheless he is keenly aware that what we know—or think we know—can lure us from resting in God's wisdom and lead us toward boasting in our own.

The organ of knowledge was given to us that we might know God and how the world relates to God. One of the first things we learn when we know him as we ought is the Word of Jesus: "Flesh and blood has not revealed this to you, but my Father who is in heaven" (Matthew 16:17). All true knowing depends on God. "Who has been [God's]... For from him and through him and to him are all things" (Romans 11:34, 36). God gave us minds not only to know, but to know how we ought to know. We know the way we ought to know when we boast in the Source of all knowing, not in our fragile little chip, with its tiny, God-designed circuitry. God has not chosen many wise, says the apostle. And the reason he gives is "so that no human being might boast in the presence of God." But: "Let the one who boasts, boast in the Lord" (1 Corinthians 1:29, 31).

When we boast in our wisdom we show that we have turned from God to trust in ourselves. We disclose that our satisfaction is not first in God's infinite, primary wisdom, but in our derivative, secondary capacities. It is a failure of faith in future grace—the promise of God to use his infinite wisdom to keep on managing the universe for the good of all who hope in him.

## BLOWING THE BUBBLE
## OF OUR RESOURCES

Similarly, we are prone to boast in our might. When God graciously blesses us, we leap to take credit for the gift—as if there were more satisfaction in blowing the bubble of our resourcefulness than in benefiting from God's. We have been duly warned in Deuteronomy 8:11–17,

> Beware...otherwise, when you have eaten and are satisfied, and have built good houses and lived in them, and when your herds and your flocks multiply, and your silver and gold multiply, and all that you have multiplies, then *your heart becomes proud*, and you forget the LORD your God who brought you out from the land of Egypt, out of the house of slavery... In the wilderness He fed you manna which your fathers did not know, *that He might humble you* and that He might test you, to do good for you in the end. Otherwise, you may say in your heart, "*My power and the strength of my hand made me this wealth.*" (NASB)

If the people built their houses and tended their flocks and gathered their gold *by faith in future grace*, it would not enter their minds to say, "My power and my strength have gotten me this wealth." When you live by faith in future grace, you know that all the products of your living are the products of grace.

## GOD WILL NOT SPARE HIS GLORY WITH THE PROUD

The king of Assyria illustrates the pride that rises in the heart when both wisdom and power conspire to lure the heart from God to self. God made the king the rod of his righteous wrath against the people of Israel (Isaiah 10:5). Yet the king did not delight in God's enabling power and guidance, but took credit for himself and said, "By the strength of my hand I have done it, and by my wisdom, for I have understanding; I remove the boundaries of peoples, and plunder their treasures; like a bull I bring down those who sit on thrones" (Isaiah 10:13). This is not smart. God will not share his glory with the proud. In fact, he promises, "I will punish the fruit of the arrogant heart of the king of Assyria and the pomp of his haughtiness." (Isaiah 10:12, NASB). The antidote to the king's pride is to believe this threat and find his gladness in God's power and God's wisdom, not his own.

## WHEN THE PROUD EAT GRASS LIKE AN OX

Not too much later in Israel's history the king of Babylon, Nebuchadnezzar, was brought low for his proud boast: "Is not this great Babylon, which I have built by my mighty power as a royal residence and for the glory of my majesty?" (Daniel 4:30). For that pride, God humbled him and made him eat grass like an ox in the open field (Daniel 4:33), until he learned to exult in God's sovereign power far above his own:

> All the inhabitants of the earth are accounted as nothing, and he does according to his will among the host of heaven and among the inhabitants of the earth; and none can stay his hand or say to him, "What have you done?"... Now I, Nebuchadnezzar, praise and extol and honor the King of heaven, for all his works are right and his ways are just; and those who walk in pride he is able to humble. (Daniel 4:35, 37)

The antidote to Nebuchadnezzar's pride was not merely a new knowledge in the head, but a new exultation in the heart. His praise and exultation reveal the wakening of faith, and the gladness that God ruled the future with the omnipotent grace to establish his plan and humble the proud. He was satisfied with God's prerogative to do as he pleases in the sovereign freedom of his justice and grace.

## WHY BOAST AS IF IT WERE NOT A GIFT?

Alongside wisdom and might, perhaps the greatest tempter to pride is money. With it we can purchase the resources of intelligence and power that we may not have in ourselves. So wealth is the great symbol of self-sufficiency. If we have savvy in the stock market or luck in the lottery, it makes up for any lack of other skills or power, because now we control the resources to satisfy our desires—so we think. And the result is described by God in Hosea 13:6, "As they had their pasture, they became satisfied, and being satisfied, their heart became proud; therefore, they forgot Me" (NASB). Pride is an issue of where your *satisfaction* is. "As they had their pasture, they became *satisfied*." Which is another way of saying, pride is an issue of what you are trusting in for your future. Hence, God uses the language of trust to indict Israel's pride in Jeremiah 49:4, "Why do you boast of your valleys, O faithless daughter, who *trusted in her treasures*, saying, 'Who will come against me?'"

Israel trusts in treasures to make her future secure from invading armies. Her faith is not in God's future grace. And that's the problem. She has been lured into a delusion of false delights: treasures, which themselves are gifts of God's grace. Therefore, they will pierce the hand if they lean on them instead of God. The apostle Paul would ask these people, as he did the Corinthians, "What do you have that you did not receive? If then you received it, why do you boast as if you did not receive it?" (1 Corinthians 4:7). Everything we have we have received from God. It lies in his hand to leave or to take, to turn for us or against us.

This is why the Bible never tires of telling us, "The king is not saved by his great army; a warrior is not delivered by his great strength. The war horse is a false hope for salvation, and by its great might it cannot rescue" (Psalm 33:16–17). You can buy armies and warriors and horses with your wealth, but unless the Lord decides to give you deliverance and victory, they will be useless in the day of battle. Future grace, not military force, is the final hope of kings and warriors—and everyone else. That's why the next verses in Psalm 33 point to an alternative treasure for our trust: "Behold, the eye of the LORD is on those who fear him, on those who hope in his steadfast love.... [H]e is our help and our shield. For our heart is glad in him, because we trust in his holy name" (Psalm 33:18, 20–21). This trust that looks away from our own resources and rests in God is what I mean by faith in future grace. This is the remedy for pride.

## THE ULTIMATE PRIDE: ATHEISM

When you take all three categories of temptation to self-reliance—wisdom, might, and riches—they form a powerful inducement toward the ultimate form of pride, namely, atheism. The safest way to stay supreme in our own estimation is to deny anything above us. This is why the proud preoccupy themselves with looking down on others. "A proud man is always looking down on things and people: and, of course, as long as you are looking down, you cannot see something that is above you."[10] But to preserve pride it may be simpler to proclaim that there is nothing above to look at. "In the *pride* of his face the wicked does not seek him; all his thoughts are, 'There is no God'" (Psalm 10:4). Ultimately, the proud must persuade themselves that there is no God.

One reason for this is that God's reality is overwhelmingly intrusive in all the details of life. Pride cannot tolerate the intimate involvement of God in running even the ordinary affairs of life. For example, James, the brother of Jesus, diagnoses pride behind the simple presumption of planning to go from one city to another:

Come now, you who say, "Today or tomorrow we will go into such and such a town and spend a year there

and trade and make a profit"—yet you do not know
what tomorrow will bring. What is your life? For you
are a mist that appears for a little time and then van-
ishes. Instead you ought to say, "If the Lord wills, we
will live and do this or that." As it is, you boast in
your arrogance. All such boasting is evil. So whoever
knows the right thing to do and fails to do it, for him
it is sin. (James 4:13–17)

Pride does not like the sovereignty of God. Therefore, pride
does not like the existence of God, because God is sovereign. It
might express this by saying, "There is no God." Or it might
express it by saying, "I am driving to Atlanta for Christmas."
James says, "Don't be so sure." Instead say, "If the Lord wills,
we shall live and we shall get to Atlanta for Christmas." James'
point is that God rules over whether we get to Atlanta, and
whether you live to the end of this page. "If the Lord wills, we
will live...." This is extremely offensive to the self-sufficiency
of pride—not even to have control over whether you get to
the end of the page without having a stroke!

James says that not believing in the sovereign rights of
God to manage the details of your future is arrogance. The
way to battle this arrogance is to yield to the sovereignty of
God in all the details of life, and rest in his infallible promises to show himself mighty on our behalf (2 Chronicles
16:9), to pursue us with goodness and mercy every day
(Psalm 23:6), to work for those who wait for him (Isaiah
64:4), and to supply us with all we need to live for his glory
(Hebrews 13:21). In other words, the remedy for pride is
unwavering faith in future grace.

## THE ITCH OF SELF-REGARD AND
## THE SCRATCH OF APPROVAL

One of the manifestations of pride that shows its aversion to faith in future grace is the craving it produces for human approval. C. S. Lewis explains how this craving works:

> The pleasure of pride is like the pleasure of scratching. If there is an itch one does want to scratch; but it is much nicer to have neither the itch nor the scratch. As long as we have the itch of self-regard we shall want the pleasure of self-approval; but the happiest moments are those when we forget our precious selves and have neither but have everything else (God, our fellow humans, animals, the garden and the sky) instead....[11]

The itch of self-regard craves the scratch of self-approval. That is, if we are getting our pleasure from feeling self-sufficient, we will not be satisfied without others' seeing and applauding our self-sufficiency. Hence Jesus' description of the scribes and Pharisees: "They do all their deeds to be seen by others.... [A]nd they love the place of honor at feasts and the best seats in the synagogues and greetings in the marketplaces and being called rabbi by others" (Matthew 23:5–7).

## THE VOID OF SELF-SUFFICIENCY

This is ironic. Self-sufficiency should free the proud person from the need to be made much of by others. That's what "sufficient" means. But evidently there is a void in this so-called self-sufficiency. The self was never designed to satisfy itself or rely upon itself. It never can be sufficient. We are but images of God, not the real thing. We are shadows and echoes. So there will always be an emptiness in the soul that struggles to be satisfied with the resources of self.

This empty craving for the praise of others signals the failure of pride and the absence of faith in future grace. Jesus saw the terrible effect of this itch for human glory. He named it in John 5:44, "How can you *believe*, when you receive glory from one another and do not seek the glory that comes from the only God?" The answer is, You can't. Itching for glory from other people makes faith impossible. Why? Because faith is being satisfied with all that God is for you in Jesus; and if you are bent on getting the satisfaction of your itch from the scratch of others' acclaim, you will turn away from Jesus. But if you would turn from self as the source of satisfaction (= repentance), and come to Jesus for the enjoyment of all that God is for us in him (= faith), then the itch would be replaced by a well of water springing up to eternal life (John 4:14).

## THE IRONY OF WEAK PRIDE

The irony of this insatiable itch in the self-sufficient soul becomes even more evident when pride cannot get what it wants and begins to flounder in weakness. This calls for discernment. Weak pride is not easily recognized. It sounds like an oxymoron—like round squares. But it is not. Consider the relationship between boasting and self-pity.

Both are manifestations of pride. Boasting is the response of pride to success. Self-pity is the response of pride to suffering. Boasting says, "I deserve admiration because I have achieved so much." Self-pity says, "I deserve admiration because I have sacrificed so much." Boasting is the voice of pride in the heart of the strong. Self-pity is the voice of pride in the heart of the weak. Boasting sounds self-sufficient. Self-pity sounds self-sacrificing.

The reason self-pity does not look like pride is that it appears to be needy.

But the need arises from a wounded ego and the desire of the self-pitying is not really for others to see them as helpless, but heroes. The need self-pity feels does not come from a sense of unworthiness, but from a sense of unrecognized worthiness. It is the response of unapplauded pride.[12]

When pride is not strong, it begins to worry about the future. In the heart of the proud, anxiety is to the future what self-pity is to the past. What did not go well in the past gives us a sense that we deserve better. But if we could not make things go our way in the past, we may not be able to in the future either. Instead of making the proud humble, this possibility makes them anxious.

## THE CAMOUFLAGED PRIDE OF ANXIETY

Here is another irony. Anxiety does not look like pride. It looks weak. It looks as though you admit you don't control the future. Yes, in a sense the proud admit that. But the admission does not kill pride until the proud heart is willing to look to the one who does control the future and rest in him. Until then, the proud are hanging onto their right of self-sufficiency even as it crumbles on the horizon of the future.

The remarkable biblical evidence for this is found in two places. The first is Isaiah 51:12–13 where God indicts anxious Israel by showing them the pride beneath their fear: "I, I am he who comforts you; *who are you that you are afraid of man who dies*, of the son of man who is made like grass, and have forgotten the LORD, your Maker, who stretched out the heavens and laid the foundations of the earth, and you fear continually all the day because of the wrath of the oppressor, when he sets himself to destroy?" In other words, "Who do you think you are to be afraid of mere men? You must really think you are somebody to be afraid like this!" Now that is an odd rebuke. But the meaning is plain: Your fear of man is a form of pride.

Why is anxiety about the future a form of pride? God gives the answer: "I—the Lord, your Maker—I am He who comforts you, who promises to take care of you; and those who threaten you are mere men who die. So your fear must mean that you do not trust me. You must think that your protection hangs on you. And even though you are not sure that your own resources will take care of you, yet you opt for fragile self-reliance, rather than faith in future grace. So all your trembling—weak as it is—reveals pride." The remedy? Turn from self-reliance to God-reliance, and put your faith in the all-sufficient power of future grace.

The second place where we see anxiety as a form of pride is 1 Peter 5:6–7. "Humble yourselves, therefore, under the mighty hand of God so that at the proper time he may exalt you, casting all your anxieties on him, because he cares for you." Notice the grammatical connection between verses 6 and 7. "Humble yourselves...under the mighty hand of God... *casting* all your anxieties on him." Verse 7 is not a new sentence. It's a subordinate clause. "Humble yourselves... [by] *casting* all your anxieties on him." This means that casting your anxieties on God is a way of humbling yourself under God's mighty hand. It's like saying, "Eat politely...*chewing* with your mouth shut." "Drive carefully...*keeping* your eyes open." "Be generous...*inviting* someone over on Thanksgiving."

Similarly, "Humble yourselves...*casting* your anxieties on God." One way to be humble is to cast your anxieties on God. Which means that one *hindrance* to casting your anxieties on God is pride. Which means that undue worry is a form of pride. Now why is casting our anxieties on the Lord the opposite of pride? Because pride does not like to admit that it has any anxieties. And if pride has to admit it, it still does not like to admit that the remedy might be trusting someone else who is wiser and stronger. In other words, pride is a form of unbelief and does not like to trust in future grace. Faith admits the need for help. Pride won't. Faith banks on God to give help. Pride won't. Faith casts anxieties on God. Pride won't. Therefore, the way to battle the unbelief of pride is to admit freely that you have anxieties, and to cherish the promise of future grace in the words, "He cares for you."

We end this chapter with a final glimpse at the counsel of God through Jeremiah. At the beginning of the chapter we heard him say, "Let not the wise man boast in his wisdom, let not the mighty man boast in his might, let not the rich man boast in his riches." We close by hearing him finish that sentence: "'But let him who boasts boast in this, that he understands and knows me, that I am the LORD who practices steadfast love, justice, and righteousness in the earth. For in these things I delight, declares the LORD" (Jeremiah 9:23–24). When all is said and done, that is the rock-bottom biblical answer to the question how to best fight pride. Be stunned and satisfied that we know God—and that he knows us.

I made the following entry in my journal on December 6, 1988. It's my own confession of need and my response to Jeremiah's exhortation.

Is not the most effective way of bridling my delight in being made much of, to focus on making much of God? Self-denial and crucifixion of the flesh are essential, but O how easy it is to be made much of even for my self-denial! How shall this insidious motive of pleasure in being made much of be broken except through bending all my faculties to delight in the pleasure of making much of God!

Christian hedonism[13] is the final solution. It is deeper than death to self. You have to go down deeper into the grave of the flesh to find the truly freeing stream of miracle water that ravishes you with the taste of God's glory. Only in that speechless, all-satisfying admiration is the end of self.

This "all-satisfying admiration" of all that God is for us in Jesus is what I mean by faith in future grace.

*I am not ashamed,*
*for I know whom I have believed,*
*and I am convinced that he is able to guard*
*until that Day what has been entrusted to me.*

2 TIMOTHY 1:12

*Everyone who believes in him*
*will not be put to shame.*

ROMANS 10:11

*Chapter Three*

# BATTLING MISPLACED SHAME

T hough shame has been fashionable as a prevalent diagnosis for emotional dysfunction, its roots are deep in the human condition, and the pain it can bring is real. If we are to live the kind of free and radically loving and holy lives Christ calls us to, we must understand the place of shame and how to fight against its crippling effects.

We start with a definition: Shame is a painful emotion caused by a consciousness of guilt or shortcoming or impropriety.[14] The pain is caused not merely by our own failures but by the awareness that others see them. Let me illustrate each of these causes.

## THREE CAUSES OF SHAME

First, consider *guilt* as a cause. Suppose you act against your conscience and withhold information on your tax returns. For a couple years you feel nothing because it has been put out of your mind, and you weren't caught. Then you are called to account by the IRS and it becomes public knowledge that you lied and you stole. Your guilt is known to your church and your employer and friends. Now in the light of public censure you feel the pain of shame.

Or take *shortcoming* as a cause. In the Olympics, suppose you come from a country where you are quite good in the 3000-meter race, compared to your countrymen. Then you compete before thousands of people in the Olympics, and the competition is so tough that by the time the last lap comes up you are a whole lap behind everyone else, and you must keep running all by yourself while everyone watches. There's no guilt here. You have done nothing wrong. But, depending on your frame of mind, the humiliation and shame could be intense.

Or consider *impropriety* as a cause of shame. You are invited to a party and you find out when you get there that you dressed all wrong. Again, there's no evil or guilt. Just a social blunder, an impropriety that makes you feel foolish and embarrassed. This too is a kind of shame.

One of the things that jumps right out at you from this definition of shame is that there is some shame that is justified, and some that isn't. There are some situations where shame is exactly what we should feel. And there are some situations where we shouldn't. Most people would say that the liar *ought* to be ashamed. And most people would probably say that the long distance runner who gave it his best shot ought *not* to feel ashamed. Disappointment would be healthy, but not shame.

## TWO KINDS OF SHAME

Let me illustrate from Scripture these two kinds of shame. The Bible makes very clear that there is a shame we ought to have and a shame we ought not to have. I'm going to call the one kind "misplaced shame" and the other kind "well-placed shame." Like everything else that matters, the crucial issue is how God fits into the experience of shame.

### Misplaced Shame

*Misplaced shame* (the kind we ought *not* to have) is the shame you feel when there is no good reason to feel it. Biblically that means that the thing you feel ashamed of is not dishonoring to God; or that it *is* dishonoring to God, but you didn't have a hand in it. In other words, misplaced shame is shame for something that's good—something that doesn't dishonor God. Or it's shame for something that's bad, but which you didn't have any sinful hand in. That's the kind of shame we ought not to have.

### Well-placed Shame

*Well-placed shame* (the kind we *ought* to have) is the shame we feel when there is good reason to feel it. Biblically that means we feel ashamed of something because our involvement in it was dishonoring to God. We ought to feel shame when we have a hand in bringing dishonor upon God by our attitudes or actions.

I want to be sure you see how important *God* is in this distinction between misplaced shame and well-placed shame. Whether we have a hand in honoring God or dis-honoring God makes all the difference. If we want to battle shame at the root, we have to know how it relates to God. And we *do* need to battle shame at the root—all shame. Because both misplaced shame and well-placed shame can cripple us if we don't know how to deal with them at the root.

It will help us in our battle, if we look at some Scriptures that illustrate misplaced shame and some that illustrate well-placed shame. We need to see that these are, in fact, biblical categories. In this day, when psychology has a tremendous influence on how we use words, we need to be sure that we can assess all language about our emotions with biblical ways of thinking and speaking. If you have learned your use of the word "shame" from contemporary psychology, be aware that I am not using it in the same way (see note 14). You may find that the Bible uses the concept of shame differently from the way it is popularly used. Once you see the biblical terms clearly, you will be in a position to assess the way contemporary people talk about shame.

## BIBLICAL EXAMPLES OF MISPLACED SHAME

Paul says to Timothy that if he feels shame for testifying to the gospel, he feels misplaced shame. "Do not be ashamed of the testimony about our Lord, nor of me his prisoner, but share in suffering for the gospel by the power of God" (2 Timothy 1:8). We ought not to feel shame for the gospel. Christ is honored when we speak well of him. And he is dishonored by fearful silence. So it is not a shameful thing to testify, but a shameful thing not to.

The same verse says that if we feel shame that a friend of ours is in prison for Jesus' sake, then our shame is misplaced. The world may see imprisonment for Christ as a sign of weakness and defeat. But Christians know better. God is honored by the courage of his servants to go to prison for his name, if they have acted in just and loving ways. We ought not to feel shame that we are associated with something that honors God in this way, no matter how much scorn the world heaps on us.

In a well-known saying of Jesus, we learn that our shame is misplaced when we feel shame because of who Jesus is or what he says. "Whoever is ashamed of me and of my words in this adulterous and sinful generation, of him will the Son of Man also be ashamed when he comes in the glory of his Father with the holy angels" (Mark 8:38). For example, if Jesus says, "Love your enemies," and others laugh and call it unrealistic, we should not feel ashamed. If Jesus says, "Don't fornicate," and promiscuous people label this command out-of-date, we should not feel shame to stand with Jesus. That would be misplaced shame because the words of Jesus are true and God-honoring, no matter how foolish the world may try to make them look.

Suffering and being reproached and made fun of as a Christian is not an occasion for shame, because it is an occasion for glorifying God. "If anyone suffers as a Christian, let him not be ashamed, but let him glorify God in that name" (1 Peter 4:16). In other words, in the Bible the criterion for what is well-placed shame and what is misplaced shame is not how foolish or how bad you look to men, but whether you in fact bring honor to God.

## WHOSE HONOR IS AT STAKE IN OUR SHAME?

This is extremely important to grasp, because much of what makes us feel shame is not that we have brought dishonor to God by our actions, but that we have failed to give the appearance that other people admire. Much of our shame is not God-centered but self-centered. Until we get a good handle on this, we will not be able to battle the problem of shame at its root.

A lot of Christian shame comes from what man thinks rather than what God thinks. But if we realized deeply that God's assessment is infinitely more significant than anyone else's, we would not be ashamed of things that are so amazing they are even called the very power of God: "I am not ashamed of the gospel, for it is the power of God for salvation to everyone who believes" (Romans 1:16). This verse tells us another reason that shame in the gospel would be misplaced shame. The gospel is the very power of God for salvation. The gospel magnifies God and humbles man. To the world the gospel doesn't look like power at all. It looks like weakness—asking people to be like children and telling them to depend on Jesus, instead of standing on their own two feet. But for those who believe, it is the power of God to give sinners everlasting glory.

One of the reasons we are tempted to feel shame even at the power of Jesus is that Jesus shows his power in ways that the world does not recognize as powerful. Jesus said to Paul in 2 Corinthians 12:9, "My grace is sufficient for you, for my power is made perfect in weakness." Paul responds to this strange demonstration of power, "I will boast all the more gladly of my weaknesses, so that the power of Christ may rest upon me. For the sake of Christ, then, I am content with weaknesses, insults, hardships, persecutions, and calamities. For when I am weak, then I am strong" (2 Corinthians 12:9–10). Ordinarily weaknesses and insults are occasions for shame. But for Paul they are occasions for exultation. Paul thinks that shame in his weaknesses and shame at his persecutions would be misplaced shame. Why? Because the power of Christ is perfected in Paul's weakness.

I conclude from this—and from all these texts—that the biblical criterion for misplaced shame is radically God-centered. The biblical criterion says, Don't feel shame for something that honors God, no matter how weak or foolish it makes you look in the eyes of unbelievers.

## BIBLICAL EXAMPLES OF
## WELL-PLACED SHAME

The same God-centeredness is seen when we look at passages that illustrate well-placed shame. Paul says to the Corinthians who were doubting the resurrection, "Wake up from your drunken stupor, as is right, and do not go on sinning. For some have no knowledge of God. I say this to your shame" (1 Corinthians 15:34). Here Paul says that these people *ought* to feel shame. "I say this to your shame." Their shame would be well-placed if they saw their deplorable ignorance of God and how it was leading to false doctrine (no resurrection) and sin in the church. In other words, well-placed shame is shame for what dishonors God—like ignorance of God, and sin against God, and false beliefs about God.

In the same church, some of the believers were going to secular courts to settle disputes among themselves. Paul rebukes them. "I say this to your shame. Can it be that there is no one among you wise enough to settle a dispute between the brothers?" (1 Corinthians 6:5). Again he says they should feel shame: "I say this to your shame." Their shame would be well-placed because their behavior is bringing such disrepute on their God. They are disputing with one another before godless judges to settle their disputes. A well-placed shame is the shame you feel because you are involved in dishonoring God.

These people were trying their best to appear strong and right. They wanted to be vindicated by men. They wanted to be winners in court. They didn't want anyone to run over them, as though they had no rights. That would look weak and shameful. So in the very act of wanting to avoid shame, as the world sees it, they fell into the very behavior that God counts shameful. The point is: When you are dishonoring God, you ought to feel shame, no matter how strong or wise or right you are in the eyes of the world.

When a Christian's eyes are opened to the God-dishonoring evil of his former behavior, he rightly feels ashamed. Paul says to the Roman church, "When you were slaves of sin, you were free in regard to righteousness. But what fruit were you getting at that time from the things of which you are now ashamed? The end of those things is death" (Romans 6:20–21). There is a proper place for looking back and feeling the twinge of pain that we once lived in a way that was so belittling to God. We will see in a moment that we are not to be paralyzed by dwelling on this. But a sensitive Christian heart cannot think back on the follies of youth and not feel echoes of the shame, even if we have settled it all with the Lord.

Well-placed shame can be very healthy and redemptive. Paul said to the Thessalonians, "If anyone does not obey what we say in this letter, take note of that person, and have nothing to do with him, that he may be *ashamed*" (2 Thessalonians 3:14). This means that shame is a proper and redemptive step in conversion and in a believer's repentance from a season of spiritual coldness and sin. Shame is not something to be avoided at all costs. There is a place for it in God's good dealings with his people.

We can conclude from what we have seen so far that the biblical criterion for misplaced shame and for well-placed shame is radically God-centered. The biblical criterion for *misplaced shame* says, *Don't* feel shame for something that honors God, no matter how weak or foolish or wrong it makes you look in the eyes of other people. And don't take onto yourself the shamefulness of a truly shameful situation unless you are in some way truly woven into the evil. The biblical criterion for *well-placed shame* says, *Do* feel shame for having a hand in anything that dishonors God, no matter how strong or wise or right it makes you look in the eyes of men.

## BATTLING THE UNBELIEF OF MISPLACED SHAME

Now comes the crucial question that relates to living by faith in future grace. How do you battle this painful emotion called shame? The answer is: We battle it at the root—by battling the unbelief that feeds its life. We fight for faith in the promises of God that overcome shame and relieve us from its pain. I'll try to illustrate this battle with three instances.

## FUTURE GRACE FOR A FORGIVEN HARLOT

First, in the case of well-placed shame, the pain ought to *be* there, but it ought not to *stay* there. If it does, it's owing to a lack of faith in the promises of God. For example, a woman comes to Jesus in a Pharisee's house weeping and washing his feet. No doubt she felt shame as the eyes of Simon communicated to everyone present that this woman was a sinner and that Jesus had no business letting her touch him. Indeed, she was a sinner. There was a place for true shame. But not for too long. Jesus said, "Your sins are forgiven" (Luke 7:48). And when the guests murmured about this, he helped her faith again by saying, "Your faith has saved you; go in peace" (Luke 7:50).

How did Jesus help her battle the crippling effects of shame? He gave her a promise: "Your sins are forgiven! Your faith has saved you. Your future will be one of peace." He declared that past pardon would now yield future peace. So the issue for her was faith in this future grace rooted in the authority of Jesus' forgiving work and freeing word. Would she believe the glowering condemnation of the guests? Or would she believe the reassuring words of Jesus that her shame was over—that she is now and in the future forgiven, that she may go in peace and wholeness and freedom? Whom will she trust? With whose promise will she satisfy her soul?

That is the way every one of us must battle the effects of a well-placed shame that threatens to linger too long and cripple us. We must battle unbelief by taking hold of the promises of future grace and peace that come through the forgiveness of our shameful acts. "With you there is forgiveness, that you may be feared" (Psalm 130:4). "Seek the LORD while he may be found; call upon him while he is near; let the wicked forsake his way, and the unrighteous man his thoughts; let him return to the LORD, that he may have compassion on him, and to our God, for he will abundantly pardon" (Isaiah 55:6–7). "If we confess our sins, he is faithful and just to forgive us our sins and to cleanse us from all unrighteousness" (1 John 1:9). "Everyone who believes in him receives forgiveness of sins through his name" (Acts 10:43).

It doesn't matter whether the act of God's forgiveness is entirely past, or if there is new forgiveness in the future[15]—in both cases the issue is the liberating power of God's forgiveness for our *future*—freedom from shame. Forgiveness is full of future grace. When we live by faith in future grace, we are freed from the lingering, paralyzing effects of well-placed shame.

## UNASHAMED, FOR I KNOW WHOM I HAVE BELIEVED

The second instance of battling shame is when we feel shame for something that is not even bad—like Jesus or the gospel. Second Timothy 1:12 shows how Paul battled against this misplaced shame. He says, "I am not ashamed, for I know whom I have believed, and I am convinced that he is able to guard until that Day what has been entrusted to me."

Paul makes very clear here that the battle against misplaced shame is a battle against *unbelief*. "I am not ashamed, for I know whom I have believed," and I am confident of his keeping power. We fight against feelings of shame in Christ and the gospel and the Christian lifestyle by fighting for faith in the future grace of God. Do we really believe that the gospel is the power of God unto salvation? Do we believe that Christ's power is made perfect in our weakness? Do we really believe that endless glory awaits us in place of ridicule? Do we believe he will keep us for that great day? The battle against misplaced shame is the battle to live by faith in the greatness and glory of future grace.

## FREED FROM SHAME THAT IS NOT OURS TO BEAR

Finally, we battle shame when others try to load us with shame for evil circumstances, when in fact we had no part in dishonoring God. This is extremely common. I would guess that the most common psychological diagnosis of people's emotional disorders is that they grew up in "shame-based families." There are some detailed and sophisticated connotations of meaning in this phrase that I would not affirm. But the understanding of misplaced shame I am developing here, and the one implied in the phrase "shame-based families" overlap. There is such a thing as shame that is repeatedly put on people, but which does not belong to them. Freeing people who have been hurt deeply by carrying this misplaced shame is also what living by faith in future grace is meant to do.

It has been a great encouragement to me to realize that this kind of "shaming" happened to Jesus repeatedly. For example, they called him a drunkard and a glutton (Luke 7:34). They called him a temple destroyer (Mark 14:58). They called him a hypocrite: He saved others, but he can't save himself (Luke 23:35). In all this, the goal was to load Jesus with a shame that was not his to bear. They hoped they could discourage him and paralyze him by heaping shameful accusations on him.

The same was true in Paul's experience. They called him mad when he defended himself in court (Acts 26:24). They called him an enemy of the Jewish customs and a breaker of the Mosaic law (Acts 21:21). They said he taught that you should sin so that grace may abound (Romans 3:8). His enemies said this to load him with a shame that it was not his to bear.

And it has no doubt happened to you, perhaps from immature parents, and probably from others. And it will happen again. How do we battle this misplaced shame? We battle it by believing the promises of God that in the end all the efforts to put us to shame will fail. We may struggle now to know what is our shame to bear and what is not. But God has a promise for us that covers either case. Isaiah promises the people who trust in God, "You shall not be put to shame or confounded to all eternity" (Isaiah 45:17). And Paul applies the Old Testament promise to Christians: "Everyone who believes in him will not be put to shame" (Romans 10:11).

In other words, for all the evil and ridicule and criticism that others may use to make us feel shame, and for all the distress and emotional pain that it brings, nevertheless the promise of God stands sure: They will not succeed in the end. All the children of God will be vindicated. The truth will be known. And no one who banks his hope on the promises of God will be put to shame. Living by faith in future grace is a life of freedom from crippling shame.

*Judge not the Lord by feeble sense,*
*But trust him for his grace.*
*Behind a frowning providence*
*He hides a smiling face.*

WILLIAM COWPER

*Be patient, therefore, brothers,*
*until the coming of the Lord....*
*As an example of suffering and patience,*
*brothers, take the prophets who spoke*
*in the name of the Lord.*
*Behold, we consider those blessed*
*who remained steadfast.*
*You have heard of the steadfastness of Job,*
*and you have seen the purpose of the Lord,*
*how the Lord is compassionate and merciful.*

JAMES 5:7–11

*The LORD is good to those who wait for him.*

LAMENTATIONS 3:25

*Chapter Four*

---

# BATTLING
# IMPATIENCE

### IN GOD'S PLACE, AT GOD'S PACE,
### BY FUTURE GRACE

Impatience is a form of unbelief. It's what we begin to feel when we start to doubt the wisdom of God's timing or the goodness of God's guidance. It springs up in our hearts when our plan is interrupted or shattered. It may be prompted by a long wait in a checkout line or a sudden blow that knocks out half our dreams. The opposite of impatience is not a glib denial of loss. It's a deepening, ripening, peaceful willingness to wait for God in the unplanned place of obedience, and to walk with God at the unplanned pace of obedience—to wait in his place, and go at his pace. And the key is faith in future grace.

## MARIE DURANT'S
## UNBENDING COMMITMENT

In his book, *Passion*, Karl Olsson tells a story of incredible patience among the early French Protestants called Huguenots.

> In the late Seventeenth Century in...southern France, a girl named Marie Durant was brought before the authorities, charged with the Huguenot heresy. She was fourteen years old, bright, attractive, marriageable. She was asked to abjure the Huguenot faith. She was not asked to commit an immoral act, to become a criminal, or even to change the day-to-day quality of her behavior. She was only asked to say, "J'abjure." No more, no less. She did not comply. Together with thirty other Huguenot women she was put into a tower by the sea.... For thirty-eight years she continued.... And instead of the hated word *J'abjure* she, together with her fellow martyrs, scratched on the wall of the prison tower the single word *Resistez*, resist!
>
> The word is still seen and gaped at by tourists on the stone wall at Aigues-Mortes.... We do not understand the terrifying simplicity of a religious commitment which asks nothing of time and gets nothing from time. We can understand a religion which enhances time.... But we cannot understand a faith which is not nourished by the temporal hope that tomorrow things will be better. To sit in a prison room with thirty others and to see the day change into night and summer into autumn, to feel the slow

systemic changes within one's flesh: the drying and wrinkling of the skin, the loss of muscle tone, the stiffening of the joints, the slow stupefaction of the senses—to feel all this and still to persevere seems almost idiotic to a generation which has no capacity to wait and to endure.[16]

Patience is the capacity to "wait and to endure" without murmuring and disillusionment—to wait in the unplanned place, and endure the unplanned pace. Karl Olsson uses one key adjective that points to the power behind patience. He said, "We cannot understand a faith which is not nourished by the *temporal* hope that tomorrow things will be better." I wonder if we can understand such patience. Surely we cannot, if "temporal" hope is the only kind we have. But if there is a hope beyond this temporal life—if future grace extends into eternity—then there may be a profound understanding of such patience in this life.

In fact, it is precisely the hope of future grace beyond this life that carries the saints patiently through their afflictions. Paul made this crystal clear in his own life: "We do not lose heart [that is, we don't succumb to murmuring and impatience]. Though our outer nature is wasting away, our inner nature is being renewed day by day. For this slight momentary affliction is preparing for us an eternal weight of glory beyond all comparison, as we look not to the things that are seen but to the things that are unseen. For the things that are seen are *transient*, but the things that are unseen are *eternal*" (2 Corinthians 4:16–18). I do not doubt that it was just this faith in future grace—beyond the temporal—that sustained the patience of Marie Durant and gave her the strength for thirty-eight years to write *Resistez* on the wall of her cell.

## THE INNER STRENGTH OF PATIENCE

Strength is the right word. The apostle Paul prayed for the church at Colossae, that they would be "*strengthened* with all power, according to his glorious might, for all *endurance and patience*" (Colossians 1:11). Patience is the evidence of an inner strength. Impatient people are weak, and therefore dependent on external supports—like schedules that go just right and circumstances that support their fragile hearts. Their outbursts of oaths and threats and harsh criticisms of the culprits who crossed their plans do not sound weak. But that noise is all a camouflage of weakness. Patience demands tremendous inner strength.

For the Christian, this strength comes from God. That is why Paul is praying for the Colossians. He is asking God to empower them for the patient endurance that the Christian life requires. But when he says that the strength of patience is "according to [God's] glorious might" he doesn't just mean that it takes divine power to make a person patient. He means that faith in this glorious might is the channel through which the power for patience comes. Patience is indeed a fruit of the Holy Spirit (Galatians 5:22) but the Holy Spirit empowers (with all his fruit) through "hearing with faith" (Galatians 3:5).[17] Therefore, Paul is praying that God would connect us with the "glorious might" that empowers patience. And that connection is faith.

## TRUSTING GOD TO MAKE ALL
## BARRIERS BLESSINGS

Specifically the glorious might of God that we need to see and trust is the power of God to turn all our detours and obstacles into glorious outcomes.

If we believed that our hold-up at the long red light was God's keeping us back from an accident about to happen, we would be patient and happy. If we believed that our broken leg was God's way of revealing early cancer in the x-ray so that we would survive, we would not murmur at the inconvenience. If we believed that the middle-of-the-night phone call was God's way of waking us to smell smoke in the basement, we would not grumble at the loss of sleep. The key to patience is faith in the future grace of God's "glorious might" to transform all our interruptions into rewards.

In other words, the strength of patience hangs on our capacity to believe that God is up to something good for us in all our delays and detours. This requires great faith in future grace, because the evidence is seldom evident. There is a legend told by Richard Wurmbrand which illustrates the necessity of believing God for good, unseen purposes, when all we can see is evil and frustration.

A legend says that Moses once sat near a well in meditation. A wayfarer stopped to drink from the well and when he did so his purse fell from his girdle into the sand. The man departed. Shortly afterwards another man passed near the well, saw the purse and picked it up. Later a third man stopped to assuage his thirst and went to sleep in the shadow of the well. Meanwhile, the first man had discovered that his purse was missing and assuming that he must have lost it at the well, returned, awoke the sleeper (who of course knew nothing) and demanded his money back. An argument followed, and irate, the first man slew the latter. Where upon Moses said to God, "You see, therefore men do not believe you. There is too much evil and injustice in the world. Why should the first man have lost his purse and then become a murderer? Why should the second have gotten a purse full of gold without having worked for it? The third was completely innocent. Why was he slain?" God answered, "For once and only once, I will give you an explanation. I cannot do it at every step. The first man was a thief's son. The purse contained money stolen by his father from the father of the second man, who finding the purse only found what was due him. The third was a murderer whose crime had never been revealed and who received from the first the punishment he deserved. In the future believe that there is sense and righteousness in what transpires even when you do not understand."[18]

Moses' impatience with God in this story would surely be overcome if he had more faith in God's power and wisdom to turn all things for the good of his people. God has promised again and again in the Bible to do just that (2 Chronicles 16:9; Psalm 23:6; 84:11; Jeremiah 32:40–41; Isaiah 64:4; Romans 8:28, 32; 1 Corinthians 3:22–23). Not every implication in this legend is faithful to the Scriptures. For example, it is an overstatement to put in the mouth of God the words, "For once and only once, I will give you an explanation." The fact is: God has given us explanations like this repeatedly in the Bible with enough illustrations to fill a book.

## KEY TO PATIENCE:
## "GOD MEANT IT FOR GOOD"

For example, the story of Joseph in Genesis 37–50 is a great lesson in why we should have faith in the sovereign future grace of God. Joseph is sold into slavery by his brothers, which must have tested his patience tremendously. But he is given a good job in Potiphar's household. Then, when he is acting uprightly in the unplanned place of obedience, Potiphar's wife lies about his integrity and has him thrown into prison—another great trial to his patience. But again things turn for the better and the prison-keeper gives him responsibility and respect. But just when he thinks he is about to get a reprieve from the Pharaoh's cupbearer, whose dream he interpreted, the cupbearer forgets him for two more years. Finally, the meaning of all these detours and delays becomes clear. Joseph says to his long-estranged brothers, "God sent me before you to preserve for you a remnant on earth, and to keep alive for you many survivors.... As for you, you meant evil against me, but God meant it for good, to bring it about that many people should be kept alive, as they are today" (Genesis 45:7; 50:20).

What would have been the key to patience for Joseph during all those long years of exile and abuse? The answer is:

faith in future grace—the sovereign grace of God to turn the unplanned place and the unplanned pace into the happiest ending imaginable.

## A HONEYMOON TRAGEDY

Not everybody's story turns out so well in this life. Benjamin Warfield was a world-renowned theologian who taught at Princeton Seminary for almost thirty-four years until his death on February 16, 1921. Many people are aware of his famous books, like *The Inspiration and Authority of the Bible*. But what most people don't know is that in 1876, at the age of twenty-five, he married Annie Pierce Kinkead and took a honeymoon to Germany. During a fierce storm Annie was struck by lightning and permanently paralyzed. After caring for her for thirty-nine years, Warfield laid her to rest in 1915. Because of her extraordinary needs, Warfield seldom left his home for more than two hours at a time during all those years of marriage.[19]

Now here was a shattered dream. I recall saying to my wife the week before we married, "If we have a car accident on our honeymoon, and you are disfigured or paralyzed, I will keep my vows, 'for better or for worse.'" But for Warfield it actually happened. She was never healed. There was no kingship in Egypt at the end of the story—only the spectacular patience and faithfulness of one man to one woman through thirty-eight years of what was never planned—at least, not planned by man. But when Warfield came to write his thoughts on Romans 8:28, he said, "The fundamental thought is the universal government of God. All that comes to you is under His controlling hand. The secondary thought is the favour of God to those that love Him. If He governs all, then nothing but good can befall those to whom He would do good.... Though we are too weak to help ourselves and too blind to ask for what we need, and can only groan in unformed longings, He is the author in us of these very longings...and He will so govern all things that we shall reap only good from all that befalls us."[20]

## NOT EVEN DEATH IS A DECISIVE INTERRUPTION

This is true even in the case of death. Some saints die in prison (Revelation 2:10). But even death becomes the servant of God's children. This is what Paul meant when he said, "All things are yours, whether...the world or life or death...all are yours, and you are Christ's, and Christ is God's" (1 Corinthians 3:21–23). As our possession, death serves us; it exists for our benefit. Another way of saying this is that death cannot separate us from the love of God, but that in it—as in "distress, or persecution, or famine, or nakedness, or danger, or sword"—"we are more than conquerors through him who loved us" (Romans 8:35–37). Even if we die we conquer. And death ends up serving our best interest.[21]

So the lesson of Joseph—and the whole Bible—stands: When delays and detours and frustrations and opposition ruin our plans and bode ill for us, faith in future grace lays hold on the sovereign purpose of God to bring something magnificent to pass. That is the key to patience.

## THE PATH OF FAITHFUL PATIENCE
## IS NOT A STRAIGHT LINE

Another great lesson in how the sovereignty of God's grace leads to patience is the story of how the temple was rebuilt after the Babylonian exile. The way God turns things around is so amazing he must have been smiling. Israel had been in exile for decades. Now the time had come, in God's planning, for their restoration to the promised land. How could this happen? That was, no doubt, the question in many Jewish minds as they struggled to be patient with God's timing. The answer is that God is sovereign over emperors' wills. Ezra tells us that "in the first year of Cyrus king of Persia, that the word of the LORD by the mouth of Jeremiah might be fulfilled, the LORD stirred up the spirit of Cyrus king of Persia...to build him a house at Jerusalem" (Ezra 1:1–2). This is absolutely astonishing. Out of the blue, God moves the heart of Cyrus to pay attention to this little people called the Jews, and send them off to Jerusalem to rebuild their temple. Who would have dreamed it could happen this way? Perhaps those who have faith in future grace. But the best is yet to come.

Over 42,000 Jewish refugees return and start building the temple in Jerusalem. Imagine the joy. But beware. The path of faithfulness is seldom a straight line to glory. Their enemies in Judah oppose them and discourage them. "Then the people of the land discouraged the people of Judah and made them afraid to build and bribed counselors against them to frustrate their purpose, all the days of Cyrus king of Persia, even until the reign of Darius king of Persia" (Ezra 4:4–5). Imagine the frustration and impatience of the people.

God had seemingly opened the door to rebuild the temple, and now there was paralyzing opposition.

But God had a different plan. Oh, for people with faith in future grace to see what mere physical eyes cannot see! Yes, the people of the land had stopped the building. But can we not trust God that the same sovereignty that moved Cyrus also prevails over the local opponents? We are so slow to learn the lesson of God's sovereign grace! In Ezra 5:1 God sends two prophets, Haggai and Zechariah, to inspire the people to begin building again. Of course, the enemies are still there. They try again to stop the building of the temple. They write a letter to Darius, the new emperor. But it backfires entirely, and now we see why God had allowed the building to cease temporarily.

Instead of agreeing with the letter and stopping the temple-building, Darius searches the archives and finds the original decree from Cyrus which authorized the building of the temple. The result is stunning. He writes back the news—beyond what they could ask or think. He says to the enemies in Judah, "Let the work on this house of God alone.... Moreover, I make a decree regarding what you shall do for these elders of the Jews for the rebuilding of this house of God. *The cost is to be paid to these men in full and without delay from the royal revenue*" (Ezra 6:7–8). In other words, God ordained a setback for a season, so that the temple would not only be built but *paid for* under Darius! If faith could apprehend this kind of future grace, would not impatience be conquered?

And lest we doubt that this was really all a plan of God, Ezra 6:22 states the great fact plainly: "the LORD had made them joyful and had turned the heart of the king of Assyria to them, so that he aided them in the work of the house of God, the God of Israel" If William Cowper (1731–1800) had already written his great hymn, "God Moves in a Mysterious Way," I think the people of Israel would have been singing it.

> *Judge not the Lord by feeble sense,*
> *But trust him for his grace,*
> *Behind a frowning providence*
> *He hides a smiling face.*

Living by faith in future grace means believing that "the king's heart is a stream of water in the hand of the LORD; he turns it wherever he will" (Proverbs 21:1). God did it to Cyrus (Ezra 1:1); he did it to Darius (Ezra 6:22) and he did it later to Artaxerxes: "Blessed be the LORD, the God of our fathers, who *put such a thing as this into the heart of the king*, to beautify the house of the LORD" (Ezra 7:27). God is ruling the world. He is ruling history. And it is all for the good of his people and the glory of his name. "From of old no one has heard or perceived by the ear, no eye has seen a God besides you, who *acts for those who wait for him*" (Isaiah 64:4). The power of patience flows through faith in the future, sovereign grace of God.

## THE LORD IS COMPASSIONATE AND MERCIFUL

We have stressed that this grace is "sovereign." We also need to stress that it is grace. It is merciful and full of good will toward

us. This is what James stresses about Job's experience of suffering, and his struggle with impatience. James commands us to
be patient and gives us the key:

> Be patient, therefore, brothers, until the coming of
> the Lord. See how the farmer waits for the precious
> fruit of the earth, being patient about it, until it
> receives the early and the late rains. You also, be
> patient. Establish your hearts, for the coming of the
> Lord is at hand. Do not grumble against one another,
> brothers, so that you may not be judged; behold, the
> Judge is standing at the door. As an example of suf-
> fering and patience, brothers, take the prophets who
> spoke in the name of the Lord. Behold, we consider
> those blessed who remained steadfast. You have
> heard of the steadfastness of Job, and you have seen
> *the purpose of the Lord, how the Lord is compassionate
> and merciful.* (James 5:7–11)

James wants us to see the purpose of Job's suffering. The
word for "purpose" is *telos* and means "goal." It was God's
goal in all his dealings with Job to be merciful, and fit him for
a greater blessing. This is what Job had missed and why he
repented from his murmuring the way he did: "Therefore I
despise myself, and repent in dust and ashes" (Job 42:6). The
power of patience flows from faith in this truth: In all his
dealings with us his goal "is compassionate and merciful."
Faith in future grace is faith in grace that is sovereign, and
sovereignty that is gracious.

## THROUGH FAITH AND PATIENCE
## WE INHERIT THE PROMISES

Patience is sustained by faith in the promise of future grace. In every unplanned frustration on the path of obedience God's Word holds true: "I will not turn away from doing good to them…. I will rejoice in doing them good, and I will plant them in this land in faithfulness, with all my heart and all my soul" (Jeremiah 32:40–41). He is pursuing us with goodness and mercy all our days (Psalm 23:6). Impatient complaining is therefore a form of unbelief.

Which is why the command to be patient takes on such immense significance. Jesus said, "By your [patient] *endurance* you will gain your lives" (Luke 21:19). And the writer to the Hebrews said, "[Be] imitators of those who through faith and patience inherit the promises" (Hebrews 6:12). We come into our inheritance on the path of patience, not because patience is a work of the flesh that earns salvation, but because patience is a fruit of faith in future grace.

We need to constantly remind ourselves that we are saved *for* good works, not *by* good works. "By grace you have been saved through faith. And this is not your own doing; it is the gift of God, *not a result of works*, so that no one may boast. For we are his workmanship, created in Christ Jesus *for good works*, which God prepared beforehand, that we should walk in them" (Ephesians 2:8–10). Faith alone unites us to Christ who is our perfect righteousness before God. In this righteous standing, which we have by faith alone, we are given the Holy Spirit to help us *endure* to the end in growing likeness to Christ. This endurance in patient and imperfect obedience is necessary (since fruit proves the reality of faith and union with Christ), but it is not the ground of our right standing with God. Christ is. Because of this confidence and all it implies for our future, we endure through hard times.

Charles Simeon was in the Church of England from 1782 to 1836 at Trinity Church in Cambridge. He was appointed to his church by a bishop against the will of the people. They opposed him, not because he was a bad preacher, but because he was an evangelical—he believed the Bible and called for conversion and holiness and world evangelization.

For twelve years the people refused to let him give the Sunday afternoon sermon. And during that time they boy-cotted the Sunday morning service and locked their pews so that no one could sit in them. He preached to people in the aisles for twelve years! The average stay of a pastor in America is less than four years. Simeon began with twelve years of intense opposition—and lasted fifty-four years. How did he endure in such patience?

> In this state of things I saw no remedy but faith and patience [Note: the linking of faith and patience!]. The passage of Scripture which subdued and con-trolled my mind was this, "The servant of the Lord must not strive." [Note: The weapon in the fight for faith and patience was the Word!] It was painful indeed to see the church, with the exception of the aisles, almost forsaken; but I thought that if God would only give a double blessing to the congrega-tion that did attend, there would on the whole be as much good done as if the congregation were doubled

and the blessing limited to only half the amount. This comforted me many, many times, when without such a reflection, I should have sunk under my burden.[22]

Where did he get the assurance that if he followed the way of patience there would be a blessing on his work that would make up for the frustrations of having all the pews locked? He got it from texts that promised future grace—texts like Isaiah 30:18, "Blessed are all those who wait for [the Lord]." The Word conquered unbelief, and faith in future grace conquered impatience.

Fifty-four years later he was dying. It was October, 1836. The weeks dragged on, as they have for many dying saints. I've learned, beside many dying believers, that the battle with impatience can be very intense on the death bed. On October 21, those by his bed heard him say these words slowly and with long pauses:

> Infinite wisdom has arranged the whole with infinite love; and infinite power enables me—to rest upon that love. I am in a dear Father's hands—all is secure. When I look to Him, I see nothing but faithfulness—and immutability—and truth; and I have the sweetest peace—I cannot have more peace.[23]

The reason Simeon could die like that is because he had trained himself for fifty-four years to go to Scripture and to take hold of the promises of future grace and use them to conquer the unbelief of impatience. He had learned to use the sword of the Spirit to fight the fight of faith in future grace. By faith in future grace he had learned to wait with God in the unplanned *place* of obedience, and to walk with God at the unplanned pace of obedience. With the psalmist he said, "I *wait* for the LORD, my soul *waits*, and *in his word I hope*" (Psalm 130:5). In his living and dying, Charles Simeon makes plain and powerful the promise, "The LORD is good to those who wait for him" (Lamentations 3:25).

*Keep your life free from love of money,*
*and be content with what you have, for he has said,*
*"I will never leave you nor forsake you."*
*So we can confidently say,*
*"The Lord is my helper;*
*I will not fear; what can man do to me?"*

HEBREWS 13:5–6

*I have learned in whatever situation I am to be content.*
*I know how to be brought low,*
*and I know how to abound.*
*In any and every circumstance,*
*I have learned the secret of facing plenty and hunger,*
*abundance and need.*
*I can do all things through him who strengthens me.*

PHILIPPIANS 4:11–13

*There is great gain in godliness with contentment.*

1 TIMOTHY 6:6

---

# Chapter Five

# BATTLING COVETOUSNESS

## THE BIG PICTURE

Let's keep the big, strategic picture clear as we focus in these chapters on the various tactical battles of the Christian life. The aim of this book is to fix in our minds this truth: The way to fight sin in our lives is to battle our bent toward unbelief. We are prone to drift away from a hearty confidence in who Christ is, what he has done for us, and all the promises that are sure because of Christ. We must never let go of the blood and righteousness of Christ as the ground of our right standing with God and guarantee of all God's promises. By faith in Christ, we embrace him as our righteousness and we embrace all that God promises to be for us in him. The fulfillment of those promises, grounded in the work of Christ, is what I mean by future grace. This is the way we fight sin. Or to put it positively, the way we pursue righteousness and love is to fight for faith in future grace.

## WHY FIGHT FOR FAITH
## IN FUTURE GRACE?

There is a practical holiness without which we will not see the Lord. "Strive for peace with everyone, and for the holiness without which no one will see the Lord" (Hebrews 12:14). Many live as if this were not so. There are professing Christians who live such unholy lives that they will hear Jesus' dreadful words, "I never knew you; depart from me, you workers of lawlessness" (Matthew 7:23). There are church-attending people who believe they are saved because they once prayed to receive Jesus, not realizing that the genuineness of that experience is proved by endurance: "The one who *endures to the end* will be saved" (Matthew 24:13). Paul says to professing believers, "If you live according to the flesh you will die" (Romans 8:13). So there is a holiness without which no one will see the Lord. And learning to fight for holiness by faith in future grace is supremely important.

A second reason for stressing this particular strategy in fighting our sin is that there is another way to pursue holiness that backfires and leads to death. What a tragedy, that I might persuade you from Scripture that there is a holiness without which we will not see the Lord—only to have you start fighting for it in a way that is denounced in Scripture and doomed to failure!

The apostles warn us against serving God any other way than by faith in his enabling grace. For example, Peter says, "Whoever serves, [let him do so] as one who serves by *the strength that God supplies*—in order that in everything God may be glorified through Jesus Christ" (1 Peter 4:11). And

Paul says, "I will not venture to speak of anything except what *Christ has accomplished through me*" (Romans 15:18; cf. 1 Corinthians 15:10). Moment by moment, grace arrives to enable us to do "every good work" that God appoints for us. "And God is able to make all *grace* abound to you, so that having all sufficiency in all things at all times, you may abound in *every good work*" (2 Corinthians 9:8). The fight for good works is a fight to believe in this future grace.

A third reason for this focus on fighting for faith in future grace is that I long for God to be glorified in our pursuit of holiness and love. But God is not glorified unless our pursuit is empowered by faith in his promises. And the God who revealed himself most fully in Jesus Christ, who was crucified for our sins and raised for our justification (Romans 4:25), is most glorified when we embrace his promises with joyful firmness because they are bought by the blood of his Son.

God is honored when we are humbled for our feebleness and failure, and when he is trusted for future grace (Romans 4:20). So unless we learn how to live by faith in future grace, we may perform remarkable religious rigors, but not for God's glory. He is glorified when the power to be holy comes from humble faith in future grace. Martin Luther said, "[Faith] honors him whom it trusts with the most reverent and highest regard, since it considers him truthful and trustworthy."[24] The trusted Giver gets the glory.

My great desire is that we learn how to live for God's honor. And that means living by faith in future grace, which, in turn, means battling unbelief in all the ways it rears its head, including covetousness.

## What Is Covetousness?

Amazingly, of all sins, covetousness ranks high enough—or low enough—to be explicitly forbidden in the Ten Commandments: "You shall not covet" (Exodus 20:17). There's a good clue to its meaning in 1 Timothy 6:5–6. It speaks of "people who are depraved in mind and deprived of the truth, imagining that godliness is a means of gain. Now there is great gain in godliness with contentment." The word "covetousness" isn't used here but the reality is what this text is all about. When verse 5 says that some are treating godliness as a means of gain, Paul responds in verse 6 that "there is great gain in godliness with contentment." This gives us the key to the definition of covetousness.

*Covetousness is desiring something so much that*
*you lose your contentment in God.*
*The opposite of covetousness is contentment in God.*

When contentment in God decreases, covetousness for gain increases. That's why Paul says in Colossians 3:5 that covetousness is idolatry. "Put to death...what is earthly in you: sexual immorality, impurity, passion, evil desire, and *covetousness, which is idolatry.*" It's idolatry because the contentment that the heart should be getting from God, it starts to get from something else.

So covetousness is desiring something so much that you lose your contentment in God or losing your contentment in God so that you start to seek it elsewhere.

Have you ever considered that the Ten Commandments

begin and end with virtually the same commandment—"You shall have no other gods before me" (Exodus 20:3) and "You shall not covet" (Exodus 20:17)? These are almost equivalent commands. Coveting is desiring anything other than God in a way that betrays a loss of contentment and satisfaction in him. Covetousness is a heart divided between two gods. So Paul calls it idolatry.

## FLEE COVETOUSNESS, FIGHT FOR FAITH

In 1 Timothy 6:6–12, Paul is trying to persuade and empower people not to be covetous. But let's be sure that we see how Paul understands this battle against covetousness. He gives reasons for not being covetous in verses 6–10 (which we will come back to). Then, in verse 11 he tells Timothy to flee the love of money and the desire to be rich. "O man of God, flee these things." Instead of giving in to covetousness, he continues, "Pursue righteousness, godliness, *faith*, love, steadfastness, gentleness." Then out of that list he picks "faith" for special attention, and says in verse 12, "Fight the good fight of the faith." In essence, then, he says, "Flee covetousness...fight the good fight of faith."

In other words, the fight against covetousness is nothing other than the fight of faith in future grace.

## THE FIGHT FOR CONTENTMENT, THAT IS, FAITH IN FUTURE GRACE

When you stop and think about it, that's just what the definition of covetousness implies. I said that covetousness is desiring something so much that you lose your contentment in God or losing your contentment in God so that you start to seek contentment elsewhere. But this contentment in God is just what faith is.

Jesus said in John 6:35, "I am the bread of life; whoever comes to me shall not hunger, and whoever *believes* in me shall never thirst."[25] In other words, what it means to believe in Jesus is to experience him as the satisfaction of my soul's thirst and my heart's hunger. Faith is the experience of contentment in Jesus. The fight of faith is the fight to keep your heart contented in Christ—to really believe, and keep on believing, that he will meet every need and satisfy every longing.

## GRATITUDE FOR GIFTS YOU ARE CONTENT WITHOUT

Paul said that this was not only a fight to be fought (1 Timothy 6:12) but a secret that had to be learned. "*I have learned* in whatever situation I am to be content.... In any and every circumstance, *I have learned the secret* of facing plenty and hunger, abundance and need" (Philippians 4:11–12). The force of Paul's testimony here comes out more clearly if we see why he wrote it to the Philippians. He is writing this fourth chapter of Philippians to thank the church for their financial generosity to him. But Paul had been blistered with criticism more than once for having ulterior motives in his ministry—that he really wanted people's money, not their salvation (see 1 Corinthians 9:4–18; 2 Corinthians 11:7–12; 12:14–18; 1 Thessalonians 2:5, 9; Acts 20:33). So he is skittish about giving any impression that he is eager to get their money.

How does he deflect that suspicion? Twice he says, "Thanks, but...." In Philippians 4:10–11 he says, "I rejoiced in the Lord greatly that now at length you have revived your (financial) concern for me.... *Not that* I am speaking of being in need." In other words, my joy in your giving is not because I have lost my contentment. On the contrary, "I have learned in whatever situation I am to be content. I know how to be brought low, and I know how to abound." To deflect the criticism that he is covetous for their gifts, he says that his gratitude for their gifts does not come from discontent.

He does the very same thing in the next paragraph (Philippians 4:15–17). He praises them for being the only church that has repeatedly sent him support. "You Philippians yourselves know that...no church entered into partnership with me in giving and receiving, except you only.... *Not that* I seek the gift, but I seek the fruit that increases to your credit." Here again: "Thanks, but...." He deflects the accusation of covetousness. "I am glad you support me, but...don't misunderstand. If it sounds like I am seeking your gifts, that's a mistake."

Only this time, instead of saying that he has learned to be content without their gifts (vv. 11–12), he says that the cause of his joy is *their* benefit, not his. "I seek the fruit that increases to your credit." *They* are the richer for their generosity, not just Paul. As Jesus said, they have been laying up for themselves treasures in heaven by being generous to the needy (Luke 12:33).

So, after his first expression of thanks, he says, "Don't

misunderstand, I'm not discontent" (see Philippians 4:11). And after his second expression of thanks he says, "Don't misunderstand, what I really seek is that you be blessed" (see Philippians 4:17). This shows that love is the flip side of contentment. Love "seeketh not her own" (1 Corinthians 13:5, KJV). It seeks the good of the neighbor (1 Corinthians 10:24). This is what Paul was doing. "Not that I seek the gift, but I seek the fruit that increases to your credit." Where did this impulse of love come from? It came from contentment. "I have learned in whatever situation I am to be content." Therefore, what I seek is not the gift that comes to me in receiving, but the benefit that comes to you in giving. Contentment is the cause of love.

## I CAN DO ALL THINGS THROUGH CHRIST, INCLUDING HUNGER

And where does this contentment come from? Philippians 4:13 gives the answer: "I can do *all things* through him who strengthens me." God's provision of day-by-day future grace enables Paul to be filled or to be hungry, to prosper or suffer, to have abundance or go wanting. "I can do all things" really means "all things," not just easy things. "All things" means, "Through Christ I can hunger and suffer and be in want." This puts the stunning promise of verse 19 in its proper light: "My God will supply every need of yours according to his riches in glory in Christ Jesus." What does "all your needs" mean in view of Philippians 4:14? It means "all that you need for God-glorifying contentment." Paul's love for the Philippians flowed from his contentment in God, and his contentment flowed from his faith in the future grace of God's infallible provision.

It's obvious then that covetousness is exactly the opposite of faith. It's the loss of contentment in Christ so that we start to crave other things to satisfy the longings of our heart. And there's no mistaking that the battle against covetousness is a battle against unbelief and a battle for faith in future grace. Whenever we sense the slightest rise of covetousness in our hearts we must turn on it and fight it with all our might using the weapons of faith.

## WE MUST BELIEVE THE WARNINGS TOO

Paul saw clearly that the main fuel for faith is the Word of God—promises such as, "My God will supply...." So when covetousness begins to raise its greedy head, what we must do is begin to preach the Word of God to ourselves. We need to hear what God says. We need to hear his warnings about what becomes of the covetous and how serious it is to covet. And we need to hear his promises of future grace that give great contentment to the soul, and free us to love.

Consider some warnings against covetousness. Let them send you running to the covetousness-destroying promises.

### 1. Covetousness Never Brings Satisfaction.

"He who loves money will not be satisfied with money, nor he who loves wealth with his income; this also is vanity" (Ecclesiastes 5:10). God's Word on money is that it does not satisfy those who love it. If we believe him, we will turn away from the love of money. It is a dead-end street.

Jesus put it like this in Luke 12:15, "Take care, and be on your guard against all covetousness, for one's life does not

consist in the abundance of his possessions." If the Word of
the Lord needed confirming, there are enough miserable rich
people in the world to prove that a satisfied life does not
come from having things. Watch the news and see if it is not
true that just as many people commit suicide by jumping off
the Coronado Bridge in San Diego (in spite of wealth), as off
the Brooklyn Bridge in New York (because of poverty).

## 2. Covetousness Chokes Off Spiritual Life.

When Jesus told the parable of the soils (Mark 4:1–20), he
said that some seed "fell among thorns, and the thorns grew
up and choked it." Then he interpreted the parable and said
that the seed is the Word of God. The thorns choking the
seed are "the cares of the world and the deceitfulness of
riches and the desires for other things" (v. 19). Covetousness
is the "desire for other things" in competition with the Word
of God.

A real battle rages when the Word of God is preached.
"The desire for other things," can be so strong that the begin-
nings of spiritual life can be choked out altogether. This is
such a frightful warning that we should all be on our guard
every time we hear the Word to receive it with faith and not
choke it with covetousness. This is the conclusion of Jesus
after telling that parable: "Take care then how you hear"
(Luke 8:18).

## 3. Covetousness Spawns Many Other Sins.

When Paul says, "The love of money is a root of all kinds of
evils" (1 Timothy 6:10), he means that the kind of heart that
finds contentment in money and not in God is the kind of

heart that produces all other kinds of evils. James gives an example, "You covet and cannot obtain so you fight and wage war" (James 4:2, my translation). In other words, if we were content, like Paul, in hard times and easy times, we would not be driven to fight and wage war like this. Covetousness is a breeding ground for a thousand other sins. And that heightens the warning to flee from it and fight for contentment in God with all our might.

## 4. Covetousness Lets You Down When You Need Help Most.

It lets you down in the hour of death. In 1 Timothy 6:7, Paul says, "We brought nothing into the world, and we cannot take anything out of the world." At the greatest crisis of your life, when you need contentment and hope and security more than any other time, your money and all your possessions take wings and fly away. They let you down. They are fair-weather friends at best. And you enter eternity with nothing but the measure of contentment that you had in God.

If you dropped dead right now, would you take with you a payload of pleasure in God or would you stand before him with a spiritual cavity where covetousness used to be? Covetousness lets you down just when you need help most.

## 5. In the End, Covetousness Destroys the Soul.

In 1 Timothy 6:9, Paul says again, "Those who desire to be rich fall into temptation, into a snare, into many senseless and harmful desires that plunge people into ruin and destruction." In the end, covetousness can destroy the soul in hell. The reason I am sure that this destruction is not some temporary financial fiasco, but final destruction in hell, is what Paul says in verse 12. He says that covetousness is to be resisted with the fight of faith, then adds, "Take hold of the eternal life to which you were called and about which you made the good confession." What's at stake in fleeing covetousness and fighting for contentment in future grace is eternal life.

So when Paul says in 1 Timothy 6:9 that the desire to be rich plunges people into ruin, he isn't saying that greed can mess up your marriage or your business (which it certainly can!). He is saying that covetousness can mess up your eternity. Or, as verse 10 says at the end, "It is through this craving that some have wandered away from the faith and pierced themselves with many pangs" (literally: "impaled themselves with many pains").

God has gone the extra mile in the Bible to warn us mercifully that the idolatry of covetousness is a no-win situation. It's a dead-end street in the worst sense of the word. It's a trick and a trap. So my word to you is the word of 1 Timothy 6:11: Flee from it. When you see it coming (in a television ad or a Christmas catalog or an internet pop-up or a neighbor's purchase), run from it the way you would run from a roaring, starving lion escaped from the zoo. But where do you run?

## THE SWORD THAT PUTS COVETOUSNESS TO DEATH

You run to the arsenal of faith and quickly take the mantle of prayer from Psalm 119:36 and throw it around yourself: "[O Lord], *incline my heart* to your testimonies, and not to selfish gain!" In other words, "Grant me the future grace of strong influences on my heart to give me an appetite for your truth that breaks the power of my appetite for things." Without the future grace of God, our hearts will pursue money. We must pray that he will incline our hearts to his Word, where the triumph over covetousness is promised.

After putting on this mantle of prayer, we must then quickly take down two cutlasses from the armory of God's Word: a short one and a long one, specially made by the Holy Spirit to slay covetousness. And we must stand our ground at the door. When the lion of covetousness shows his deadly face we show him the shorter cutlass, namely, 1 Timothy 6:6, "There is great gain in godliness with contentment."

We preach it to our souls and thrust it at the attacking greed. "GREAT GAIN! Great gain in godliness with contentment! Stay where you are, lion of covetousness. I have great gain when I rest contented in God. He is my treasure now, and he will be to the end. This is my faith in future grace. Be gone!"

Then, if the lion persists, you take the longer cutlass (Hebrews 13:5–6), "Keep your life *free from love of money, and be content* with what you have, for he has said, 'I will never leave you nor forsake you.' So we can confidently say, 'The Lord is my helper; I will not fear; what can man do to me?'" Trusting this all-satisfying promise of future grace, you drive it into the chest of the lion of greed. You do exactly what Paul says in Colossians 3:5, "Put covetousness to death."

Brothers and sisters, all covetousness is unbelief in future grace. Learn with me, oh, learn with me how to use the sword of the Spirit to fight the good fight of faith, and lay hold on the future grace of eternal life!

*Beloved, never avenge yourselves,*
*but leave it to the wrath of God,*
*for it is written,*
*"Vengeance is mine, I will repay,*
*says the Lord."*

ROMANS 12:19

*We cannot ignore inconsiderate acts in others;*
*yet we cannot execute the penalty of law.*
*We have no right to complete the moral cycle....*
*Although we sense no spiritual inhibition against*
*crying out against injustice,*
*the purity of our moral life deteriorates the moment*
*we attempt to administer justice.*

EDWARD JOHN CARNELL

*The dark-valley breath of bitterness cannot survive the*
*high paths of faith in future grace. Grudges demand the*
*valley-vapors of self-pity and fear and emptiness. They*
*cannot survive the contentment and confidence and*
*fullness of joy that come from satisfaction in the*
*forgiving God of future grace.*

*Chapter Six*

---

# BATTLING
# BITTERNESS

## WHAT ABOUT FAITH IN FUTURE JUSTICE?

Is the judgment of God on our enemies an act of future grace toward us? This is a crucial question because the point of this book is to help us battle unbelief and defeat sin by faith in future grace. What I find in the New Testament is that one powerful way of overcoming bitterness and revenge is to have faith in the promise that God will settle accounts with our offenders so that we don't have to. The New Testament teaches that we are freed from vengeance by believing that God will take vengeance for us, if he must. So my question is this: Is believing in God's vengeance an example of faith in future *grace*, or is it only faith in future *justice*? My answer is that faith in God's judgment is another form of faith in future grace. Therefore, living by faith in future grace involves overcoming vengeance and bitterness by trusting God to settle all our accounts justly.

Ponder with me for a moment God's promise of future

justice. In Revelation 18 there is a description of God's judgment on the anti-Christian powers of the world. These powers are sometimes called "Babylon" to signify their animosity toward the people of God, and sometimes called "the great prostitute" to signify their immorality. Here is a great temptation for Christian bitterness and anger. These enemies flout the laws of God in immorality and they shed the blood of Christians. Moreover, they are impenitent to the end. In the book of Revelation, John says, "In [Babylon] was found the blood of prophets and of saints." She is "the great prostitute who corrupted the earth with her immorality, and has avenged on her the blood of his servants" (Revelation 18:24; 19:2). How should Christians respond to this immorality and persecution?

The command of Jesus in this world is "Love your enemies and pray for those who persecute you" (Matthew 5:44). The reason Jesus gives this command is "so that you may be sons of your Father who is in heaven. For he makes his sun rise on the evil and on the good" (Matthew 5:45). While life endures in this age, God gives many blessings to those who are immoral and cruel. Paul said to the Gentiles who had never heard of the true God, "[God] did not leave himself without witness, for he did good by giving you rains from heaven and fruitful seasons, satisfying your hearts with food and gladness" (Acts 14:17). In all of this, God is showing undeserved "kindness and forbearance and patience" that should lead the nations to repentance (Romans 2:4). Jesus commands us to imitate our Father in these things: "Love your enemies, and do good, and lend, expecting nothing in return, and your reward will be great, and you will be sons of the Most High, for he is kind to the ungrateful and the evil. Be merciful, even as your Father is merciful" (Luke 6:35–36).

Indeed, while there is hope for their conversion, we should feel with the apostle Paul, "My heart's desire and prayer to God for them is that they may be saved" (Romans 10:1). If we are persecuted as Christians we are to turn the other cheek (Matthew 5:39), and bless those who curse us (Luke 6:28), and not return evil for evil (1 Thessalonians 5:15; 1 Peter 3:9), but, if possible, to live in peace with all (Romans 12:17–18).

## FUTURE JUDGMENT IS
## ALSO FUTURE GRACE

But there will come a time when the patience of God is over. When God has seen his people suffer for the allotted time and the appointed number of martyrs is complete (Revelation 6:11), then vengeance will come from heaven. Paul describes it like this: "God considers it just to repay with affliction those who afflict you, and to grant relief to you who are afflicted...when the Lord Jesus is revealed from heaven with his mighty angels in flaming fire, inflicting vengeance on those who do not know God and on those who do not obey the gospel of our Lord Jesus" (2 Thessalonians 1:6–8). Notice that God's vengeance on our offenders is experienced by us as "relief." In other words, the judgment on "those who afflict" us is a form of *grace* toward us.

Jesus taught a similar truth in the parable of the unjust judge. He told the story of a widow "who kept coming to [the judge] and saying, 'Give me justice against my adversary'"

(Luke 18:3). Finally the judge relented and gave her what she needed. Jesus interprets the story: "Will not God give justice to his elect, who cry to him day and night? Will he delay long over them? I tell you, he will give justice to them speedily" (Luke 18:7-8). So again God's future justice for the opponents of his people is pictured as relief—like the relief of a widow in distress. Future justice for God's enemies is pictured as *future grace* for God's people.

Perhaps the most remarkable picture of judgment as grace is the picture of Babylon's destruction in Revelation 18. At her destruction, a great voice from heaven cries, "*Rejoice over her*, O heaven, and you saints and apostles and prophets, for God has given judgment for you against her!" (Revelation 18:20). Then a great multitude is heard saying, "*Hallelujah!* Salvation and glory and power belong to our God, for his judgments are true and just; for he has judged the great prostitute who corrupted the earth with her immorality, and has avenged on her the blood of his servants" (Revelation 19:1–2).

When God's patience has run its long-suffering course, and this age is over, and judgment comes on the enemies of God's people, the saints will not disapprove of God's justice. They will not cry out against him. On the contrary, the apostle John calls on them to "rejoice" and to shout, "Hallelujah!" This means that the final destruction of the unrepentant will not be experienced as a misery for God's people. The unwillingness of others to repent will not hold the affections of the saints hostage. Hell will not be able to blackmail heaven into misery. God's judgment will be approved and the saints will experience the vindication of truth as a great grace.

Two hundred fifty years ago Jonathan Edwards commented on Revelation 18:20 with these words: "Indeed [the saints] are not called upon to rejoice in having their revenge glutted, but in seeing justice executed, and in seeing the love and tenderness of God towards them, manifested in his severity towards their enemies."[26] This is what is stressed in Revelation 19:2, "His judgments are true and just." Thus Edwards' answer to our question is that God's final judgment is indeed a *future grace* to the people of God. He says, "It is often mentioned in Scripture, as an instance of the great love of God to his people, that his wrath is so awakened, when they are wronged and injured. Thus Christ hath promised...'if any man offend one of his little ones, it were better for him that a millstone were hanged about his neck, and that he were drowned in the depth of the sea'" (Matthew 18:6).[27]

## PROMISE: VENGEANCE IS MIND, I WILL REPAY

This future grace of God's judgment is promised to us as a means of helping us overcome a spirit of revenge and bitterness. For example, in Romans 12:19–20, Paul says, "Beloved, never avenge yourselves, but leave it to the wrath of God, for it is written, 'Vengeance is mine, I will repay, says the Lord.' To the contrary, 'if your enemy is hungry, feed him; if he is thirsty, give him something to drink; for by so doing you will heap burning coals on his head.'"

Paul's argument is that we should not take vengeance, because vengeance belongs to the Lord. And to motivate us to lay down our vengeful desires he gives us a promise— which we now know is a promise of future grace— "'I will repay,' says the Lord." The promise that frees us from an unforgiving, bitter, vengeful spirit is the promise that God will settle our accounts. He will do it more justly and more thoroughly than we ever could. Therefore, we can back off and leave room for God to work.

## IS IT WRONG TO WANT JUSTICE DONE?

Why is this such a crucial promise in overcoming our bent toward bitterness and revenge? The reason is that this promise answers to one of the most powerful impulses behind anger—an impulse that is not entirely wrong.

I can illustrate with an experience I had during my seminary days. I was in a small group for couples that began to relate at a fairly deep personal level. One evening we were discussing forgiveness and anger. One of the young wives said that she could not and would not forgive her mother for something she had done to her as a young girl. We talked about some of the biblical commands and warnings concerning an unforgiving spirit. "Be kind to one another, tenderhearted, forgiving one another, as God in Christ forgave you" (Ephesians 4:32). "If you do not forgive others their trespasses, neither will your Father forgive your trespasses" (Matthew 6:15; see also 18:34–35; Mark 11:25; Luke 17:4; 2 Corinthians 2:7). But she would not budge. I warned her that her very soul was in danger if she kept on with such an attitude of unforgiving bitterness. But she was adamant that she would not forgive her mother.

What gives so much force to the impulse of anger in such cases is the overwhelming sense that the offender does not *deserve* forgiveness. That is, the grievance is so deep and so justifiable that not only does self-righteousness strengthen our indignation, but so does a legitimate sense of moral outrage. It's the deep sense of legitimacy that gives our bitterness its unbending compulsion. We feel that a great crime would be committed if the magnitude of the evil we've experienced were just dropped and we let bygones be bygones. We are torn: Our moral sense says this evil cannot be ignored, and the Word of God says we must forgive.

## If You Hold a Grudge, You Doubt the Judge

In his penetrating book, *Christian Commitment*, Edward John Carnell described this conflict between moral outrage and forgiveness as the "judicial predicament." He said, "We cannot ignore inconsiderate acts in others; yet we cannot execute the penalty of law. We have no right to complete the moral cycle.... Although we sense no spiritual inhibition against crying out against injustice, the purity of our moral life deteriorates the moment we attempt to administer justice."[28] Nevertheless, the indignation we feel usually gets the upper hand and holds onto the offense, because it would be morally repugnant to make light of the wrong.

Now we can see why the biblical promise of God's judgment is so crucial in helping overcome this craving for revenge. It gives us a way out of the "judicial predicament." God intervenes as the avenger so that we can acknowledge the crime; but also so that we don't have to be the judge. God's promised vengeance removes the moral legitimacy of our personal craving for retaliation. God's promise says, "Yes, an outrage has been committed against you. Yes, it deserves to be severely punished. Yes, the person has not yet experienced that punishment. But, No, you may not be the one to punish, and you may not go on relishing personal retribution. Why? Because God will see to it that justice is done. God will repay. You cannot improve on his justice. He sees every angle of the evil done against you—far better than you can see it. His justice will be more thorough than any justice you could administer." If you hold a grudge, you doubt the Judge.

That's what the promise of Romans 12:19 says. And the question for the angry, offended person now becomes, "Do you believe this promise?" In other words, the issue of releasing grudges is an issue of *faith* in God's promises of future grace—the future grace of judgment on the offender. If we believe God's promise, "Vengeance is mine, I will repay," then we will not belittle God with our inferior efforts to improve upon his justice. We will leave the matter with him and live in the freedom of love toward our enemy—whether the enemy repents or not. And if he does not repent? What then? Three hundred years ago Thomas Watson said it well: "We are not bound to trust an enemy; but we are bound to forgive him."[29] We are not responsible to make reconciliation happen. We are responsible to seek it. "*So far as it depends on you, live peaceably with all*" (Romans 12:18).

## How Jesus Solved the "Judicial Predicament"

The apostle Peter shows that Jesus himself handled the "judicial predicament" in this same way. No one was more grievously sinned against than Jesus. Every ounce of animosity against him was fully undeserved. No one has ever lived who was more worthy of honor than Jesus; and no one has been dishonored more. If anyone had a right to get angry and be bitter and vengeful, it was Jesus. How did he control himself when scoundrels, whose very lives he sustained, spit in his face?

Peter gives the answer in these words: "[Jesus] committed no sin, neither was deceit found in his mouth. When he was reviled, he did not revile in return; when he suffered, he did not threaten, but *continued entrusting*[30]*...to him who judges justly*" (1 Peter 2:22–23). What this means is that Jesus had faith in the future grace of God's righteous judgment. He did not need to avenge himself for all the indignities he suffered, because he entrusted his cause to God. He left vengeance in God's hands and prayed for his enemies' repentance (Luke 23:34).

Peter gives this glimpse into Jesus' faith so that we would learn how to live this way ourselves. He said, "You have been called [to endure harsh treatment patiently] because Christ also suffered for you, *leaving you an example, so that you might follow in his steps*" (1 Peter 2:21). If Christ conquered bitterness and vengeance by faith in future grace, how much more should we, since we have far less right to murmur for being mistreated than he did.

## THE BASIS OF FORGIVING OTHER CHRISTIANS

But now another crucial question emerges. If God's promise of judgment is the basis for not holding grudges against unrepentant enemies, what is the basis of our not holding grudges against Christian brothers and sisters who do repent? Our moral indignation at a terrible offense does not evaporate just because the offender is a Christian. In fact, we may feel even more betrayed. And a simple, "I'm sorry," will often seem utterly disproportionate to the painfulness and ugliness of the offense.

But in this case we are dealing with fellow Christians and the promise of God's wrath does not apply because there is "no condemnation for those who are in Christ Jesus" (Romans 8:1). "God has not destined [Christians] for wrath, but to obtain salvation through our Lord Jesus Christ" (1 Thessalonians 5:9). So now where do we look to escape from the "judicial predicament"? Where shall we turn to assure ourselves that justice will be done—that Christianity is not a mockery of the seriousness of sin?

The answer is that we look to the cross of Christ. All the wrongs that have been done against us by *believers* were avenged in the death of Jesus. This is implied in the simple but staggering fact that *all* the sins of all God's people were laid on Jesus (Isaiah 53:6; 1 Corinthians 15:3; Galatians 1:4; 1 John 2:2; 4:10; 1 Peter 2:24; 3:18). The suffering of Christ was the recompense of God on every hurt I have ever received from a fellow Christian (Romans 4:25; 8:3; 2 Corinthians 5:21; Galatians 3:13). Therefore, Christianity does not make light of sin. It does not add insult to our injury. On the contrary, it takes the sins against us so seriously that, to make them right, God gave his own Son to suffer more than we could ever make anyone suffer for what they have done to us.

Therefore, when God says, "Vengeance is mine," the meaning is more than we may have thought. God undertakes vengeance against sin not only by means of hell, but also by means of the cross. All sin will be avenged—severely and thoroughly and justly. Either in hell, or at the cross. The sins of the unrepentant will be avenged in hell; the sins of the repentant were avenged on the cross.

What this means is that we have no need or right to harbor bitterness toward believers or unbelievers. The judicial predicament is broken. God has intervened to deliver us from the moral demand to recompense the wrongs we have endured. He has done this, in great measure, by promising, "Vengeance is mine; I will repay." If we believe him, we will not presume to take vengeance into our own hands. Rather, we will glorify the all-sufficiency of the cross and the terrible justice of hell by living in the assurance that God, and not we, will set all wrongs right. Ours is to love. God's is to settle accounts justly. And faith in future grace is the key to freedom and forgiveness.

## BYGONE GRACE:
## NECESSARY BUT NOT ENOUGH

The cross is in the past. And I am eager to affirm that the backward look to Calvary is utterly crucial for maintaining our faith in future grace. If my wife hurts me with an unkind word, I do not need to have the last word. I don't need to get even, because her sin was laid on Jesus, and he has suffered horribly to bear it for her—and for me. Jesus has taken that offense against himself and against me so seriously that he died to expose its evil and remove my wife's guilt. If this is to free me from holding a grudge, I must look back and believe that this is what happened on the cross. The backward glance is essential. The point of this book—battling unbelief and living by faith in future grace—does not nullify that.

But the backward look is not enough. What Jesus accomplished on the cross lasts forever. I must be assured of that. The grace of Calvary that consumed the sins done against me, is also the future grace that keeps me and my wife in Christ, so that the cross is effectual for us. It is future grace that promises me and my wife that if we confess our sins, God is faithful and just to forgive our sins (1 John 1:9). In other words, the past grace of the atoning cross will have to be appropriated repeatedly by future confession. And that is assured only by future grace.

## The Power of God's Forgiveness

Of course, for any who knows me and my wife, it is more likely that I will be the one needing her forgiveness more often than she needs mine. I am the one with the quick, unguarded tongue. This is why the Bible not only speaks of God's being the avenger of sins done against us, but also speaks of God's being the forgiver of sins that we do against others. This too is crucial for breaking the bondage of bitterness and freeing us to forgive.

Paul says, "Be kind to one another, tenderhearted, *forgiving one another, as God in Christ forgave you.* Therefore be imitators of God, as beloved children. And walk in love, as Christ loved us and gave himself up for us" (Ephesians

4:32–5:2). Here the power to forgive is flowing not from how God deals with the sins done against me, but from how God deals with the sins I do against others.

The battle against bitterness is fought not only by trusting the promise of God to avenge wrongs done against us; it is also fought by cherishing the experience of being forgiven by God. How does being forgiven make us forgiving people? I answer: by *faith* in our being forgiven. By *believing* that we are forgiven. But there is something perplexing here. That woman who was in the small group with me back in my seminary days would not forgive her mother, but she believed adamantly that she was forgiven. She would not let the sin of her grudge shake her security. Does faith in being forgiven then really liberate us from grudges?

What's wrong here? What's wrong is that she was apparently missing the essence of true saving faith—I say it with trembling. Saving faith is not merely believing *that* you are forgiven. Saving faith means tasting this forgiveness as part of the way God is and experiencing it (and him!) as precious and magnificent. Saving faith looks at the horror of sin, and then looks at the holiness of God, and apprehends spiritually that God's forgiveness is unspeakably glorious. Faith in God's forgiveness does not merely mean a persuasion that I am off the hook. It means savoring the truth that a forgiving God is the most precious reality in the universe. That's why I used the word "cherish." Saving faith cherishes being forgiven by God, and from there rises to cherishing the God who forgives—and all that he is for us in Jesus.

Again we see that the backward look is insufficient. The great act of forgiveness is past—the cross of Christ. By this backward look we learn of the grace in which we will ever stand (Romans 5:2). We learn that we are now and always will be loved and accepted. We learn that the living God is a forgiving God. But the great experience of being forgiven is all future. Fellowship with the great God who forgives is all future. Freedom for forgiveness flowing from this all-satisfying fellowship with the forgiving God is all future.

I have learned that it is possible to go on holding a grudge if your faith simply means you have looked back to the cross and concluded that you are off the hook. I have been forced to go deeper into what true faith is. It is being satisfied with all that God is for us in Jesus. It looks back not merely to discover that it is off the hook, but to see and savor the kind of God who offers us a future of endless reconciled tomorrows in fellowship with him.

It may be that, as you read this, no long-term grudges come to mind. Perhaps God has remarkably freed you from old hurts and disappointments and given you the grace to lay them down. But be sure to test yourself about short-term anger as well. Are there repeated present frustrations that may not have the character of long-term bitterness, but are like chronic reappearances of the same short-term anger? Are there traits of your children or your spouse or your church or your boss that week after week provoke you so deeply that you grit your teeth and rehearse in your head all the reasons why this is intolerable and should not go on? My experience has been that there is as much struggle with unbelief in these short-term, recurrent frustrations as there is in the long-term bitterness for some great abuse or betrayal. Here too we need to trust God's promises in a practical, day-by-day way.

The dark-valley breath of bitterness—short-term or long-term—cannot survive the high paths of faith in future grace. Grudges demand the valley-vapors of self-pity and fear and emptiness. They cannot survive the contentment and confidence and fullness of joy that come from satisfaction in the forgiving God of future grace.

*The greatest need of the hour is a revived*
*and joyful Church.... Unhappy Christians are,*
*to say the least, a poor recommendation*
*of the Christian faith.*

MARTYN LLOYD-JONES

*Why are you cast down, O my soul,*
*and why are you in turmoil within me?*
*Hope in God;*
*for I shall again praise him,*
*my salvation.*

PSALM 42:5

*For his anger is but for a moment,*
*and his favor is for a lifetime.*
*Weeping may tarry for the night,*
*but joy comes with the morning.*

PSALM 30:5

*Chapter Seven*

---

# BATTLING
# DESPONDENCY

*D*espondency is not a common word today. But I think
it captures what I mean. It is not *depression* per se,
because depression connotes a clinical condition in
our day. But it is more than simply having a bad day and feeling temporarily gloomy in the evening. Between those two
there is a broad terrain of unhappiness where too many
Christians live their lives. Beneath much of that experience is
unbelief in future grace of God and its foundation in the
person and work of Christ. That is the unbelief I would like
to help us battle in this chapter.[31]

## A DOCTOR OF SOULS

In 1954, one of my heroes, Martyn Lloyd-Jones, preached a
series of sermons at Westminster Chapel, London, which he
later published in a book called *Spiritual Depression*. His
assessment of the church at the middle of the twentieth century is still valid, as far as I can see. He said, "I have no
hesitation in asserting again that one of the reasons why the

Christian Church counts for so little in the modern world is that so many Christians are in this condition [of spiritual depression]."[32] "The greatest need of the hour is a revived and joyful Church.... Unhappy Christians are, to say the least, a poor recommendation of the Christian faith."[33]

Lloyd-Jones was an esteemed medical doctor before he became a preacher. This gives a special weight to his observations about the causes of despondent feelings that plague so many Christians. He is not naive about the complexity of what causes despondency. For example, he says, "There are certain people who are more prone to depression in a natural sense than others.... Though we are converted and regenerated, our fundamental personality is not changed. The result is that the person who is more given to depression than another person before conversion, will still have to fight that after conversion."[34]

## A LINEAGE OF DEPRESSION

There are many painful examples of this in the history of the church. One of the most poignant is the story of David Brainerd, the young missionary to the Indians of New England in the eighteenth century. It seems that there was an unusual strain of weakness and depression in his family. Not only did his parents die early, but David's brother Nehemiah died at 32, his brother Israel died at 23, his sister Jerusha died at 34, and he died at 29. In 1865, a descendant, Thomas Brainerd, said, "In the whole Brainerd family for two hundred years there has been a tendency to a morbid depression, akin to hypochondria."[35]

So, on top of having an austere father and suffering the loss of both parents as a sensitive child, he probably inherited some kind of tendency to depression. Whatever the cause, he suffered from the blackest dejection, off and on, throughout his short life. He says at the very beginning of his diary, "I was, I think, from my youth something sober and inclined rather to melancholy than the other extreme."[36]

Nevertheless, he said that there was a difference between the depression he suffered before and after his conversion. After his conversion there seemed to be a rock of electing love under him that would catch him, so that in his darkest times he could still affirm the truth and goodness of God, even though he couldn't sense it for a season.[37]

## THE BURDEN OF THE BODY

Not only is there the issue of hereditary temperament and personality, but there is also the issue of how physical conditions affect low moods. Lloyd-Jones says, "There are many, I find, who come to talk to me about these matters, in whose case it seems quite clear to me that the cause of the trouble is mainly physical. Into this group, speaking generally, you can put tiredness, overstrain, illness, any form of illness. You cannot isolate the spiritual from the physical for we are body, mind and spirit."[38] When the psalmist cried out, "My flesh and my heart may fail" (Psalm 73:26), he was showing us how interwoven the "heart" and the "flesh" are in the despondency he so often experienced.

Charles Haddon Spurgeon is a prime example of a great Christian and a great preacher whose recurrent despondency was almost surely owing in large measure to his painful disease of gout. It is not easy to imagine the eloquent, brilliant, full-of-energy, seemingly omnicompetent Spurgeon weeping like a baby for no reason that he could think of. In 1858, at age 24, it happened for the first time. He said, "My spirits were sunken so low that I could weep by the hour like a child, and yet I knew not what I wept for."[39] As years went by, the times of melancholy came again and again. At times he seemed ready to give up: "Causeless depression cannot be reasoned with, nor can David's harp charm it away by sweet discoursings. As well fight with the mist as with this shapeless, undefinable, yet all-beclouding hopelessness.... The iron bolt which so mysteriously fastens the door of hope and holds our spirits in gloomy prison, needs a heavenly hand to push it back."[40]

Yet he did fight. He saw his depression as his "worst feature." "Despondency," he said, "is not a virtue; I believe it is a vice. I am heartily ashamed of myself for falling into it, but I am sure there is no remedy for it like a holy faith in God."[41]

Before we look at that remedy more closely, one more complicating cause should be mentioned. There is the whole area of family conditioning. One small example: If parents reward a child for whining, and give in to the manipulation of a child's moodiness, then that child will be trained that a good pout will get pity. And thirty years later the mastery of his moods will be twice as hard.

## THE ROOT OF DESPONDENCY

What then is the root of despondency? Lloyd-Jones would agree that it is an oversimplification to say that the *single* root of despondency is unbelief. But it would be right to say, as Lloyd-Jones does say, "The *ultimate* cause of all spiritual depression is unbelief."[42] For example, where did the kind of parenting come from that sanctions pouting? Did it come from a strong *belief* in the Word of God as the best book on parenting? And why do so many people pursue nighttime activities that guarantee fatigue which leads to despondency and irritability and moral vulnerability? Is it owing to a strong *belief* in God's counsel to get good rest (Psalm 127:2) and a firm *trust* in his power to work for those who wait for him (Isaiah 64:4; Psalm 37:5)?

And could it be that brain research is in such infancy that even though we know a little bit about how chemicals can produce emotional states, we know almost nothing about the ways emotional and spiritual states may produce healing chemicals? Could anyone disprove the possibility that being satisfied with all that God is for us in Jesus has no physical effect on the body's production of natural antidepressants? Why should we not assume that the powerful affection of faith in future grace promotes even physical means of mental health? My own conviction is that when we get to heaven we will learn some astonishing things about the profound connection between sound faith and sound minds.

We may say, therefore, that the roots of despondency are not simple. They are complex. So my focus in this chapter is limited. Without denying the complexity of our emotions and their hereditary and physical and family dimensions, what I want to show is that unbelief in future grace is the root of *yielding* to despondency. Or to put it another way: Unbelief is the root of not making war on despondency with the weapons of God. Unbelief lets despondency take its course without a spiritual fight.

Lloyd-Jones said that if we are converted with a bent toward despondency we "will still have to *fight* that after conversion." It's the *fight* we are talking about in this chapter, not the onslaught of melancholy that demands the fight. Let me illustrate this from the Psalms and then from the kind of despondency that Jesus had to deal with.

## WHEN THE PSALMIST'S HEART FAILED

In Psalm 73:26, the psalmist says, "My flesh and my heart may fail." Literally, the verb is simply, "My flesh and my heart *fail!*" I am despondent! I am discouraged! But then immediately he fires a broadside against his despondency: "But God is the strength of my heart and my portion forever." The psalmist does not yield. He battles unbelief with a counterattack.

In essence, he says, "In myself I feel very weak and helpless and unable to cope. My body is shot and my heart is almost dead. But whatever the reason for this despondency, I will not yield. I will trust God and not myself. He is my strength and my portion."

The Bible is replete with instances of saints struggling with sunken spirits. Psalm 19:7 says, "The law of the LORD is perfect, *reviving the soul.*" This is a clear admission that the soul of the saint sometimes needs to be revived. And if it needs to be *revived*, in a sense it was "dead." David says the same thing in Psalm 23:2–3, "He leads me beside still waters. *He restores my soul.*" The soul of the "man after [God's] own heart" (1 Samuel 13:14) needs to be restored. It was dying of thirst and ready to fall exhausted, but God led the soul to water and gave it life again.

God has put these testimonies in the Bible so that we might use them to fight the unbelief of despondency. Wherever despondency might come from, Satan paints it with a lie. The lie says, "This is it. You will never be happy again. You will never be strong again. You will never have vigor and determination again. Your life will never again be purposeful. There is no morning after this night. No joy after weeping. All is gathering gloom, darker and darker. This is not a tunnel; it is a cave, an endless cave."

That is the color that Satan paints on our despondency. And God has woven his Word with strands of truth directly opposed to that lie. The law of God, which is now fulfilled in Jesus, *does* revive (Psalm 19:7). God *does* lead to springs of water (Psalm 23:3). God does show us the path of life (Psalm 16:11). Joy *does* come with the morning (Psalm 30:5). So the psalms illustrate for us the truth that unbelief is the root of yielding to despondency; but faith in future grace takes the promises of God and throws them against despondency. "God is the strength of my heart and my portion forever!" (Psalm 73:26).

## LEARNING TO PREACH TO OURSELVES

We must learn to fight despondency. The fight is a fight of faith in future grace. It is fought by preaching truth to ourselves about God and his promised future. This is what the psalmist does in Psalm 42. "My tears have been my food day and night, while they say to me continually, 'Where is your God?'... Why are you cast down, O my soul, and why are you in turmoil within me? Hope in God; for I shall again praise him, my salvation" (Psalm 42:3, 5). The psalmist preaches to his troubled soul. He scolds himself and argues with himself. And his main argument is future grace: "*Hope* in God!—Trust in what God will be for you in the future. A day of praise is coming. The presence of the Lord will be all the help you need. And he has promised to be with us forever" (see Psalm 23:4, 6).

Lloyd-Jones believes this issue of preaching truth to ourselves about God's future grace is all-important in overcoming spiritual depression.

> I say that we must talk to ourselves instead of allowing "ourselves" to talk to us! Do you realize what that means? I suggest that the main trouble in this whole matter of spiritual depression in a sense is this, that we allow our self to talk to us instead of talking to our self. Am I just trying to be deliberately paradoxical? Have you realized that most of your unhappiness in life is due to the fact that you are listening to yourself instead of talking to yourself? Take those thoughts that come to you the moment you wake up in the morning. You have not originated them, but they start talking to you, they bring back the problems of yesterday, etc. Somebody is talking. Who is talking to you? Your self is talking to you. Now [the psalmist's] treatment was this; instead of allowing this self to talk to him, he starts talking to himself. "Why art thou cast down, O my soul?" he asks. His soul had been depressing him, crushing him. So he stands up and says: "Self, listen

for a moment, I will speak to you.... Why art thou cast down?—what business have you to be disquieted?... And then you must go on to remind yourself of God, Who he is, and what God is and what God has done, and what God has pledged Himself to do. Then having done that, end on this great note: defy yourself, and defy other people, and defy the devil and the whole world, and say with this man: "I shall yet praise Him for the help of His countenance."[43]

The battle against despondency is a battle to believe the promises of God. And that belief in God's future grace comes by hearing the Word. And so preaching to ourselves is at the heart of the battle. But I stress again that the issue in this chapter is not mainly how to avoid meeting despondency, but how to fight it when it comes. If we go to the example of Jesus, we will see that even the sinless Son of God met and wrestled with this enemy.

## WHEN JESUS MET THE ENEMY OF DESPONDENCY

The night Jesus was betrayed he fought some deep spiritual battles. What was happening that night on the eve of our everlasting redemption was an awful spiritual war. Satan and all his strongest hosts were gathered to fight against the Son of God. And whatever Paul means by "the flaming darts of the evil one" (Ephesians 6:16), you can be sure they were flying in volleys against the heart of Jesus in Gethsemane that night.

We get a glimpse of the battle in Matthew 26:36–38:

Then Jesus went with them to a place called Gethsemane, and he said to his disciples, "Sit here, while I
go over there and pray." And taking with him Peter
and the two sons of Zebedee, he began to be *sorrowful
and troubled*. Then he said to them, "*My soul is very sorrowful, even to death*; remain here, and watch with me."

What is going on here? What is Jesus distressed about?
John 12:27 says, "Now is my soul *troubled*. And what shall I
say? 'Father, save me from this hour'? But for this purpose I have
come to this hour." In other words, the *distressing, troubling*
temptation was to despair and fail to carry out his mission. The
flaming darts coming against him were thoughts—thoughts
like, "It's not worth it. It won't work." Or perhaps just a volley
of hideous distractions. And the effect of these assaults on Jesus
was a tremendous emotional upheaval. What Satan wanted to
produce in Jesus was a spirit of despondency that would sink,
unopposed, in resignation and prompt Jesus not to carry out
what his Father had given him to do.

Now think about this for a minute. Jesus was a sinless
man (Hebrews 4:15; 2 Corinthians 5:21). This means that
the emotional turmoil he was enduring that night was a
proper and fitting response to the kind of extraordinary test-
ing he was experiencing. The demonic thought that Calvary
would be a meaningless black hole is so horrendous it *ought*
to make the soul of Christ shudder. This is the first shock-
wave of the blast of despondency. But it is not sin. Not yet.

But here is something surprising. The Gospel of John
says that Jesus was troubled (John 12:27; 13:21). The first
shockwaves of despondency broke the tranquility of his soul.

But in this same Gospel it also says that the disciples should not be troubled. In John 14:1 Jesus says, "Let not your hearts be *troubled* (same word as in 12:27 and 13:21). Believe in God; believe also in me." And in John 14:27 Jesus says, "Peace I leave with you; my peace I give to you. Not as the world gives do I give to you. Let not your hearts be *troubled*."

In both cases Jesus is dealing with the danger of despondency. The disciples were beginning to feel disheartened and hopeless because their Leader and their Friend was going away. Instead of getting brighter, things were getting darker. In both cases he said, Don't feel troubled and despondent like that.

Now, is this a contradiction? When Satan dangles the thought in front of Jesus and his disciples that their future is hopeless, is it right for Jesus to feel despondent, but not the disciples?

## LET NOT YOUR HEARTS BE TROUBLED

I don't think there's a contradiction. Here's how they fit together. Jesus was warning the disciples against *giving in* to despondency, *yielding* to it unopposed. Letting it fester and spread. And so he says, Fight back: Believe God; believe also in me (John 14:1). The first shockwaves of the blast of despondency are not the sin. The sin is in not turning on the air-raid siren, and not heading for the bomb shelters, and not deploying the antiaircraft weapons. If Satan drops a bomb on your peace, and you don't make ready for war, people are going to wonder whose side you're on.

It's just the same with Jesus. The first shockwaves of

despondency that he feels because of the assaults of temptation are not sin. But no one knew better than Jesus how
quickly they can become sin, if they are not counterattacked
immediately. You cannot read Matthew 26:36–39 and come
away saying, "Despondency's not so bad, because Jesus had it
in Gethsemane and he's sinless." Instead, what you come
away with is an impression of how earnestly he fought off the
unbelief of despondency. How much more should we!

## How Jesus Fought in the Dark Hour

There were several tactics in Jesus' strategic battle against
despondency.

First, *he chose some close friends to be with him.* "[He took]
with him Peter and the two sons of Zebedee" (Matthew
26:37). Second, *he opened his soul to them.* He said to them,
"My soul is very sorrowful, even to death" (v. 38). Third, *he
asked for their intercession and partnership* in the battle.
"Remain here, and watch with me" (v. 38). Fourth, *he poured
out his heart to his Father in prayer.* "My Father, if it be possible, let this cup pass from me" (v. 39). Fifth, *he rested his soul
in the sovereign wisdom of God.* "Nevertheless, not as I will, but
as you will" (v. 39). Sixth, *he fixed his eyes on the glorious future
grace that awaited him on the other side of the cross.* "For the joy
that was set before him [Jesus] endured the cross, despising
the shame, and is seated at the right hand of the throne of
God" (Hebrews 12:2).

When something drops into your life that seems to
threaten your future, remember this: The first shockwaves of
the bomb are not sin. The real danger is yielding to them.

Giving in. Putting up no spiritual fight. And the root of that surrender is unbelief—a failure to fight for faith in future grace. A failure to cherish all that God promises to be for us in Jesus.

Jesus shows us another way. Not painless, and not passive. Follow him. Find your trusted spiritual friends. Open your soul to them. Ask them to watch with you and pray. Pour out your soul to the Father. Rest in His sovereign wisdom. And fix your eyes on the joy set before you in the precious and magnificent promises of God.

## Don't Sit Down in the Dark

Preach to yourself that even the great apostle Paul was "afflicted in every way, but not crushed; perplexed, but not driven to despair" (2 Corinthians 4:8); that David discovered in the darkness that "[God's] anger is but for a moment, and his favor is for a lifetime. Weeping may tarry for the night, but joy comes with the morning" (Psalm 30:5). Preach to yourself what David learned in his battle with despair—that even when he says despairingly, "Surely the darkness shall cover me, and the light about me be night," nevertheless there is a greater truth: "Even the darkness is not dark to you; the night is bright as the day, for darkness is as light with you" (Psalm 139:11–12).

The final lesson of Gethsemane and Calvary and the book of the Psalms is that all the dark caves of despondency are really tunnels leading to the fields of joy—for those who don't sit down in the dark and blow out the candle of *faith in future grace.*

*He breaks the power of canceled sin.*
*He sets the prisoner free.*

CHARLES WESLEY


*If by the Spirit*
*you put to death the deeds of the body,*
*you will live.*

ROMANS 8:13


*He has granted to us his precious*
*and very great promises,*
*so that through them you may become*
*partakers of the divine nature,*
*having escaped from the corruption that*
*is in the world because of sinful desire.*

2 PETER 1:4

*Chapter Eight*

---

# BATTLING LUST

## WOULD YOU CUT OFF YOUR OWN LEG?

On July 20, 1993, Donald Wyman was clearing land near Punxsutawney, Pennsylvania, as part of his work for a mining company. In the process, a tree rolled onto his shin causing a severe break and pinning Wyman to the ground. He cried for help for an hour, but no one came. He concluded that the only way to save his life would be to cut off his leg. So he made a tourniquet out of his shoe string and tightened it with a wrench. Then he took his pocket knife and cut through the skin, muscle, and bone just below the knee and freed himself from the tree. He crawled thirty yards to a bulldozer, drove a quarter-mile to his truck, then maneuvered the manual transmission with his good leg and a hand until he reached a farmer's house one-and-a-half miles away, with his leg bleeding profusely. Farmer John Huber Jr. helped him get to a hospital where his life was spared.[44]

Jesus knew that humans love to live. So he appealed to

this passion in order to show the importance of purity. Just as Donald Wyman cut off his leg to save his life, Jesus commanded that we gouge out our eye to escape the fatal effect of lust. "Everyone who looks at a woman with lustful intent has already committed adultery with her in his heart. If your right eye causes you to sin, tear it out and throw it away. For it is better that you lose one of your members than that your whole body be thrown into hell" (Matthew 5:28–29). Of course, if you gouge out your "right eye," as Jesus says, you can still see the magazine with your left eye. So Jesus must have something even more radical in mind than literal mutilation.

## PONDER THE DANGER OF LUST

A few years ago, I spoke to a high school student body on how to fight lust. One of my points was called, "Ponder the eternal danger of lust." I quoted the words of Jesus—that it's better to go to heaven with one eye than to hell with two— and said to the students that their eternal destiny was at stake in what they did with their eyes and with the thoughts of their imagination.

I tried to counteract the prevalent notion that personal, sexual morality—including the life of the mind—is of minor moral significance. Idealistic students (and adults) often think that what they do with their bodies and their minds, on the personal level, is no big deal. If it's sin at all, it's sin with a little "s". "Shouldn't we just get on with the big issues like international peace, and global environmental strategies, and racial reconciliation, and social justice, and health-care initiatives, and the elimination of violence? Sleeping around is simply no big deal, if you are on the picket line for justice; and flipping through *Playboy* is utterly insignificant if you are on your way to peace talks in Geneva."

I stressed that Jesus sees things very differently. Those global issues are important. But the reason they are important is that they all have to do with people—not just statistical aggregates, but real individual people. And the most important thing about people is that, unlike animals and trees, they live forever in heaven glorifying God, or in hell defying God. People are not important because they breathe. They're important because they have the capacity to honor God with their hearts and minds and bodies long after they stop breathing—forever.

What Jesus is saying, therefore, is that the consequences of lust are going to be worse than the consequences of war or environmental catastrophe. The ultimate scourge of war is that it can kill the body. But Jesus said, "Do not fear those who kill the body, and after that have nothing more that they can do. But I will warn you whom to fear: fear him who, after he has killed, has authority to cast into hell. Yes, I tell you, fear him!" (Luke 12:4–5). In other words, God's final judgment is much more fearful than earthly annihilation.

## LUST AND ETERNAL SECURITY

After my message in the high school auditorium, one of the students came up to me and asked, "Are you saying then that a person can lose his salvation?" In other words, If Jesus used the threat of hell to warn about the seriousness of lust, does that mean that a Christian can perish?

This is exactly the same response I got a few years ago when I confronted a man about the adultery he was living in. I tried to understand his situation and I pled with him to return to his wife. Then I said, "You know, Jesus says that if you don't fight this sin with the kind of seriousness that is willing to gouge out your own eye, you will go to hell and suffer there forever." As a professing Christian he looked at me in utter disbelief, as though he had never heard anything like this in his life, and said, "You mean you think a person can lose his salvation?"

So I have learned again and again from firsthand experience that there are many professing Christians who have a view of salvation that disconnects it from real life, and that nullifies the threats of the Bible, and puts the sinning person who claims to be a Christian beyond the reach of biblical warnings. I believe this view of the Christian life is comforting thousands who are on the broad way that leads to destruction (Matthew 7:13). Jesus said, if you don't fight lust, you won't go to heaven. Not that saints always succeed. The issue is that we resolve to fight, not that we succeed flawlessly.

The stakes are much higher than whether the world is blown up by a thousand long-range missiles, or terrorists bomb your city, or global warming melts the icecaps, or AIDS sweeps the nations. All these calamities can kill only the body. But if we don't fight lust we lose our soul. The apostle Peter said, "Abstain from the passions of the flesh, which *wage war against your soul*" (1 Peter 2:11). The stakes in *this* war are infinitely higher than in any threat of war or terrorism. The apostle Paul listed "sexual immorality, impurity, passion, evil desire, and covetousness," then said, "On account of these the wrath of God is coming" (Colossians 3:5–6). And the wrath of God is immeasurably more fearful than the wrath of all the nations put together. In Galatians 5:19, Paul mentions immorality, impurity, and sensuality and says, "Those who do such things will not inherit the kingdom of God" (Galatians 5:21).

## JUSTIFYING FAITH IS LUST-FIGHTING FAITH

What then is the answer to this student and this man living in adultery? We are justified by grace alone through faith alone (Romans 3:28; 4:5; 5:1; Ephesians 2:8–9); and all those who are thus justified will be glorified (Romans 8:30)—that is, no justified person will ever be lost. Nevertheless, those who give themselves up to impurity will be lost (Galatians 5:21), and those who forsake the fight against lust will perish (Matthew 5:30), and those who do not pursue holiness will not see the Lord (Hebrews 12:14), and those who surrender their lives to evil desires will succumb to the wrath of God (Colossians 3:6).

The reason these two groups of texts are not contradictory is that the faith that justifies is a faith that also sanctifies. Justifying faith embraces Christ as our crucified sin-bearer and our risen righteousness before God, along with all that God promises to be for us in him. In the same way, that faith keeps on embracing Christ this way and thus becomes the means of sanctification as well as justification. The test of whether our faith is the kind of faith that justifies is whether it is the kind of faith that sanctifies. These are not two differ-ent kinds of faith. Both embrace Christ who bore our punishment, provided our righteousness, and promises to meet every need to the end of the age.

Robert Dabney, the nineteenth-century southern Presbyterian theologian, expressed it like this: "Is it by the instrumentality of faith we receive Christ as our justification, without the merit of any of our works? Well. But this same faith, if vital enough to embrace Christ, is also vital enough to 'work by love,' 'to purify our hearts.' This then is the virtue of the free gospel, as a ministry of sanctification, that the very faith which embraces the gift becomes an inevitable and a divinely powerful principle of obedience."[45]

Faith delivers from hell, and the faith that delivers from hell delivers from lust. Again I do not mean that our faith produces a *perfect flawlessness* in this life. I mean that it pro-duces a *persevering fight*. The evidence of justifying faith is that it fights lust. Jesus didn't say that lust would entirely van-ish. He said that the evidence of being heaven-bound is that we gouge out our eye rather than settle for a pattern of lust.

The main concern of this book is to show that the battle against sin is a battle against unbelief. Or: The fight for purity is a fight for faith in future grace. The great error that I am try-ing to explode is the error that says, "Faith in God is one thing and the fight for holiness is another thing. You get your justi-fication by faith, and you get your sanctification by works. You start the Christian life in the power of the Spirit, you press on in the efforts of the flesh. The battle for obedience is optional because only faith is necessary for final salvation." Faith alone is the instrument that unites us to Christ who is our righteousness and the ground of our justification. But the purity of life that confirms faith's reality is also essential for final salvation, not as the ground of our right standing, but as the fruit and evidence that we are vitally united by faith to Christ who alone is the ground of our acceptance with God.[46]

## FAITH IN FUTURE GRACE BREAKS THE POWER OF CANCELLED SIN

The battle for obedience is absolutely necessary for our final salvation, because the battle for obedience *is* the fight of faith. The battle against lust is absolutely necessary for our final salvation, because that battle *is* the battle against unbelief. I hope you can see that this is a greater gospel than the other one. It's the gospel of God's *victory* over sin, not just his *tolerance* of sin. This victory over sin is not the ground of our eternal acceptance with God. Christ is. Our sin is borne by him; his righteousness counts for us. This standing we have by faith alone before we defeat sins. Then, by this same faith and on this rock-solid position of acceptance, we put to death our sinful inclinations by the mighty grace of God. This is the gospel of Romans 6:14: "Sin will have no dominion over you, since you are not under law but under grace." Almighty grace! Sovereign grace! The kind of grace that is the future power of God to defeat the temptations of lust.

He breaks the power of canceled sin,
He sets the prisoner free;
His blood can make the foulest clean,
His blood availed for me.

Charles Wesley's hymn ("O, For a Thousand Tongues to Sing!") is right: The blood of Christ obtained for us not only the cancellation of sin, but also the conquering of sin. This is the grace we live under—the sin-conquering, not just sin-canceling, grace of God. Triumph over the sin of lust is all of grace—past grace, canceling lust's guilt through the cross, and future grace, conquering lust's power through the Spirit. That's why the only fight we fight is the fight of faith. We fight to be so satisfied with all that God is for us in Jesus that temptation to sin loses its power over us.

## How Do You Put Lust to Death?

One of the ways that Paul talks about this battle is to say, "If by the Spirit you put to death the deeds of the body, you will live" (Romans 8:13). This is close to Jesus' teaching that if we are willing to gouge out our eye rather than lust we will enter into life (Matthew 18:9). Paul agrees that eternal life is at stake in the battle against sin: "If you live according to the flesh you will die, but if by the Spirit you put to death the deeds of the body, you will live" (Romans 8:13). The fight against lust is a fight to the death.

How then do we obey Romans 8:13—to put to death the deeds of the body, to kill lust? We have answered, "By faith in future grace." But practically, what does that involve?

Suppose I am tempted to lust. Some sexual image comes into my mind and beckons me to pursue it. The way this temptation gets its power is by persuading me to believe that I will be happier if I follow it. The power of all temptation is the prospect that it will make me happier. No one sins out of a sense of duty. We embrace sin because it promises that, at least in the short run, things will be more pleasant.

So what should I do? Some people would say, "Remember God's command to be holy (1 Peter 1:16), and exercise your will to obey because he is God!" But something crucial is missing from this advice, namely, faith in future grace. A lot of people strive for moral improvement who cannot say, "The life I now live in the flesh I live by *faith* in the Son of God, who loved me and gave himself for me" (Galatians 2:20). They strive for the purity of love but don't realize that such love is the fruit of faith in future grace: "In Christ Jesus neither circumcision nor uncircumcision counts for anything, but only *faith working through love*" (Galatians 5:6).

How then do you fight lust by faith in future grace? When the temptation to lust comes, Romans 8:13 says, in effect, "If you kill it *by the Spirit*, you will live." By the Spirit! What does that mean? Out of all the armor God gives us to fight Satan, only one piece is used for killing—the sword. It is called the *sword of the Spirit* (Ephesians 6:17). So when Paul says, "Kill sin by the Spirit," I take that to mean, Depend on the Spirit, especially his sword.

What is the sword of the Spirit? It's the Word of God (Ephesians 6:17). Here's where faith comes in. "Faith comes from hearing, and hearing through the word of Christ" (Romans 10:17). This gospel Word about Christ and his saving work secures for us all the riches of Christ and his promises. This Word, therefore, cuts through the fog of Satan's lies and shows me where true and lasting happiness is to be found. And so the Word helps me stop trusting in the potential of sin to make me happy. Instead, the Word entices me to trust in God's promises.

When faith has the upper hand in my heart, I am satisfied with Christ and his promises. This is what Jesus meant when he said, "Whoever believes in me shall *never thirst*" (John 6:35). When my thirst for joy and meaning and passion are satisfied by the presence and promises of Christ, the power of sin is broken. We do not yield to the offer of sandwich meat when we can smell the steak sizzling on the grill.

The fight of faith against lust is the fight to stay satisfied with God. "By faith Moses... [forsook] the fleeting pleasures of sin. He... was looking to the reward" (Hebrews 11:24–26). Faith is not content with "fleeting pleasures." It is ravenous for joy. And the Word of God says, "In your presence there is fullness of joy; at your right hand are pleasures forevermore" (Psalm 16:11). So faith will not be sidetracked into sin. It will not give up so easily in its quest for maximum joy.

The role of God's Word is to feed faith's appetite for God. And, in doing this, it weans my heart away from the deceptive taste of lust. At first, lust begins to trick me into feeling that I would really miss out on some great satisfaction if I followed the path of purity. But then I take up the sword of the Spirit and begin to fight. I read that it is better to gouge out my eye than to lust. I read that if I think about things that are pure and lovely and excellent, the peace of God will be with me (Philippians 4:8–9). I read that setting the mind on the flesh brings death, but setting the mind on the Spirit brings life and peace (Romans 8:6). I read that lust wages war against my soul (1 Peter 2:11) and that the pleasures of this life choke out the life of the Spirit (Luke 8:14). But best of all,

I read that God withholds no good thing from those who walk uprightly (Psalm 84:11) and that the pure in heart will see God (Matthew 5:8).

As I pray for my faith to be satisfied with God's life and peace, the sword of the Spirit carves the sugar coating off the poison of lust. I see it for what it is. And by the grace of God, its alluring power is broken. I wield the sword of the Spirit against the sin of lust by believing the promise of God more than I believe in the promise of lust. My faith is not only a backward-looking belief in the death of Jesus, but a forward-looking belief in the promises of Jesus. It's not only being sure of what he *did* do, but also being satisfied with what he *will* do—indeed, it is being satisfied with what he will do precisely *because* of what he did do (Romans 8:32).

It is this Spirit-given superior satisfaction in future grace that breaks the power of lust. With all eternity hanging in the balance, we fight the fight of faith. Our chief enemy is the lie that says *sin* will make our future happier. Our chief weapon is the Truth that says God will make our future happier. And faith is the victory that overcomes the lie, because faith is satisfied with God.

## FIGHTING FIRE WITH FIRE

I have often told young people that they must fight fire with fire. The fire of lust's pleasures must be fought with the fire of God's pleasures. If we try to fight the fire of lust with prohibitions and threats alone—even the terrible warnings of Jesus—we will fail. We must fight it with a massive promise of superior happiness. We must swallow up the little flicker of lust's pleasure in the conflagration of holy satisfaction. When we "make a covenant with our eyes," like Job did (Job 31:1), our aim is not merely to avoid something erotic, but also to gain something excellent.

Peter described this powerful liberating process in 2 Peter 1:3–4. He said,

> [God's] divine power has granted to us all things that pertain to life and godliness, through the knowledge of him who called us to his own glory and excellence, by which he has granted to us his precious and very great promises, so that through them you may become partakers of the divine nature, having escaped from the corruption that is in the world because of sinful desire.

How do we escape from the corruption that comes from the "sinful desire" of lust? The answer is that God has given us a revelation of "his own glory and excellence" expressed in "precious and very great promises." These have been given to us for this very purpose: that "through them" we might share God's character and be freed from the corruption of lust. The key is the power of promises. When we are entranced by the *preciousness* of them and the *magnificence* of them, the effect is liberation from the lusts, which are, in fact, not precious and not magnificent. Paul calls these enslaving lusts, "*deceitful* desires" (Ephesians 4:22), and he says that the "passion of lust" of the Gentiles stems from the fact that they "do not know God" (1 Thessalonians 4:5). Similarly, Peter calls these lusts, "the passions of your former *ignorance*"— that is, ignorance of God's glory and his precious and magnificent promises (1 Peter 1:14). What Paul and Peter mean is that these lusts get their power by lying to us in order to deceive us. They prey upon our ignorance of the promises of God. They claim to offer precious pleasures and magnificent experiences. What can free us from them? Compelling, inspiring, enthralling Truth. The truth of God's precious and magnificent promises that expose the lie of lust in the light of God's all-surpassing glory.

## THE PURE SHALL SEE GOD

In the fall of 1982, *Leadership* magazine carried an unsigned article by a pastor who confessed to years of bondage to pornography of the grossest kind. He tells the story of what finally released him. It is a resounding confirmation of what I am trying to say. The author ran across a book by Francois Mauriac, the Catholic French novelist, *What I Believe*. In it Mauriac admitted how the plague of guilt had not freed him from lust. He concludes that there is one powerful reason to seek purity, the one Christ gave in the Beatitudes: "Blessed are the pure in heart, for they shall see God" (Matthew 5:8). It is the "precious and magnificent" promise that the pure see God that empowers our escape from lust. The lust-bound pastor wrote,

> The thought hit me like a bell rung in a dark, silent hall. So far, none of the scary, negative arguments against lust had succeeded in keeping me from it....
> But here was a description of what I was missing by continuing to harbor lust: I was limiting my own inti-

macy with God. The love he offers is so transcendent and possessing that it requires our faculties to be purified and cleansed before we can possibly contain it. Could he, in fact, substitute another thirst and another hunger for the one I had never filled? Would Living Water somehow quench lust? That was the gamble of faith.[47]

It was not a gamble. You can't lose when you turn to God. He discovered this in his own life, and the lesson he learned is absolutely right: The way to fight lust is to feed faith with the precious and magnificent promise that the pure in heart will see, face to face, the all-satisfying God of glory.

The challenge before us in our fight against lust is not merely to do what God says because He is God, but to desire what God says because he is glorious. The challenge is not merely to *pursue* righteousness, but to *prefer* righteousness. The challenge is to get up in the morning and prayerfully meditate on the Scriptures as the only place where we see the gospel of the glory of Christ. Here we meet the ground and the goal of all God's promises, Jesus Christ. He said to the Jewish leaders, "You search the Scriptures because you think that in them you have eternal life; and *it is they that bear witness about me*" (John 5:39). And Luke tells us that after his resurrection, on the Emmaus road, he pointed to himself in *all the Scriptures*—"Beginning with Moses and all the Prophets, he interpreted to them in all the Scriptures the things concerning himself" (Luke 24:27). The challenge before us is to mediate on these Christ-revealing Scriptures until we experience "joy and peace in believing" in him and his "precious and very great promises" (Romans 15:13; 2 Peter 1:4).

As faith in future grace satisfies us with the joy set before us, the biblical demand for purity of heart will not be burdensome (1 John 5:3), and the power of lust will be broken. Its deceitful compensation will appear too brief and too shallow to lure us in.

# CONCLUSION

The emphasis of this book has been different from one frequent emphasis in books on motivation for Christian obedience. A very common emphasis is that gratitude for God's past grace is the main motivation for future obedience. I have warned in the larger book from which this one comes that this is risky. It can lead, as it has for many, to thinking of obedience as repayment to God for what he has done for us. I called that mistake "the debtor's ethic."[48] When every step of obedience is sustained and enabled by ever-arriving future grace, there can be no talk of paying God back.

Nor can there be any talk of getting out of debt to his grace. On the contrary, with every breath we go deeper into debt to grace. And, praise God, it will always be so. I will never become God's benefactor. He will always be the inexhaustible giver. This must be so, for the giver gets the glory. "Whoever serves... [let him serve] by the strength that *God supplies*—in order that in everything *God may be glorified* through Jesus Christ" (1 Peter 4:11). Serving God is not payback, but more receiving. Moment by moment, as we bank on ever-arriving future grace, we go deeper and deeper into glorious debt.

Therefore, the privileged place for gratitude is huge. With every moment of dependence on the arrival of future grace, the reservoir of past grace is growing. The magnitude of this reservoir is the ground of joyful gratitude. Therefore, our thankfulness should abound more and more every day. So here at the end of this book, looking back on so much past grace, I feel drawn to pay tribute to the place of gratitude in the Christian life. It is not a small place.

## A TRIBUTE TO GRATITUDE
## FOR PAST GRACE

There are ways that gratitude helps bring about obedience to Christ. One way is that the spirit of gratitude is simply incompatible with some sinful attitudes. I think this is why Paul wrote, "Let there be no filthiness nor foolish talk nor crude joking, which are out of place, but instead *let there be thanksgiving*" (Ephesians 5:4). Gratitude is a humble, happy response to the goodwill of someone who has willed to do us a favor. This humility and happiness cannot coexist in the heart with coarse, ugly, mean attitudes. Therefore, the cultivation of a thankful heart leaves little room for such sins.

Not only that, there is a crucial relationship between the backward look of gratitude to embrace past grace and the forward look of faith to embrace future grace. They are interwoven joys that strengthen each other. As gratitude joyfully revels in the benefits of past grace, so faith joyfully relies on the benefits of future grace. Therefore, when gratitude for

God's past grace is strong, the message is sent that God is supremely trustworthy in the future because of what he has done in the past. In this way, faith is strengthened by a lively gratitude for God's past trustworthiness.

On the other hand, when faith in God's future grace is strong, the message is sent that this kind of God makes no mistakes, so that everything he has done in the past is part of a good plan and can be remembered with gratitude. In this way, gratitude is strengthened by a lively faith in God's future grace. Surely it is only the heart of faith in future grace that can follow the apostle Paul in "giving thanks *always and for everything* to God the Father in the name of our Lord Jesus Christ" (Ephesians 5:20). Only if we trust God to turn past calamities into future comfort can we look back with gratitude for *everything*.

This interwovenness of future-oriented faith and past-oriented gratitude is what prevents gratitude from degenerating into the debtor's ethic. Gratitude for bygone grace is constantly saying to faith, "Be strong, and do not doubt that God will be as gracious in the future as I know he's been in the past." And faith in future grace is constantly saying to gratitude, "There is more grace to come, and all our obedience is to be done in reliance on that future grace. Relax and exult in your appointed feast. I will, by God's grace, take responsibility for tomorrow's obedience."

## INFINITELY FULL, INFINITELY LONG, RICHES OF GRACE

What we have seen in this book is eight snapshots of "faith working through love" (Galatians 5:6). I say with the apostle

Paul that the aim of it all has been God-glorifying love that flows from faith in God's future grace: "The *aim* of our charge is love that issues from a pure heart and a good conscience and *a sincere faith*" (1 Timothy 1:5). Now in conclusion I want to simply emphasize the infinite fullness and duration of the future grace that sustains our joy and our obedience forever.

Paul speaks in Ephesians 2:7 of the "riches of [God's] grace." His point is that the free overflow of God's inexhaustible, self-replenishing fullness is immeasurably great. There is no end to grace because there is no bottom to the well from which it comes. I find it overwhelmingly amazing that God has raised us with Christ for the express purpose of lavishing on us the eternal riches of God's grace. Let this divine purpose sink into your heart: "[God] raised us up with him and seated us with him in the heavenly places in Christ Jesus, *so that in the coming ages he might show the immeasurable riches of his grace in kindness toward us in Christ Jesus*" (Ephesians 2:6–7).

There are two astonishing things here. One is that the purpose of our salvation is for God to lavish the riches of his grace on us. The other is that it will take him forever to do it. Forever—infinite futurity. This is a mighty thought. God made us alive and secured us in Christ so that he could make us the beneficiaries of everlasting kindness from infinite riches of grace. This is not because we are worthy. Quite the contrary, it is to show the infinite measure of *his* worth. Grace would not be grace if it were a response to resources in us. Grace is *grace* because it highlights God's own overflowing resources of kindness. Grace is *eternal* because it will take that long for God to expend inexhaustible stores of goodness on us. Grace is *free* because God would not be the infinite, self-sufficient God he is, if he were constrained by anything outside himself.

This shows why future grace is so utterly crucial in God's great plan to glorify himself and satisfy his people. Most of our experience of God's active grace lies in the future. The grace that we have already experienced from God is infinitesimally small compared to the future grace that we will experience from now to eternity. This will always be so, since a finite duration, of even millions of years, is small compared to the infinity of the future. Here is a treasure to be prized. This is what faith in future grace does. It prizes "the immeasurable riches of his grace in kindness toward us in Christ Jesus." Here is the great evil of unbelief. Should we not trust such a promise? Yes, we should. And we should battle every whiff of unbelief with all our might.

## ONE MORE LOOK AT THE
## LOGIC OF HEAVEN

So let us make our farewell with the reminder of the solid logic of heaven. God could not have done more to prove his resolve to lavish us with the immeasurable riches of his grace. Romans 8:32 is the great statement of God's guaranteed resolve. "He who did not spare his own Son but gave him up for us all, how will he not also with him graciously give us all things?" The impossible thing is done: the Son of God unsparingly condemned to remove our sin and provide our righteousness. Therefore, nothing, absolutely nothing, will stop God from giving us "all things" with him.

Here is a worthy tribute to this great verse from John Flavel, a Puritan pastor from over three hundred years ago. It expresses the essence and certainty of future grace:

He spared not his own Son, but delivered him up for us all; how shall he not with him freely give us all things?" (Romans 8:32). How is it imaginable that God should withhold, after this, spiritual [blessings] or temporal [blessings] from his people? How shall he not call them effectually, justify them freely, sanctify them thoroughly, and glorify them eternally? How shall he not clothe them, feed them, protect and deliver them? Surely if he would not spare this own Son one stroke, one tear, one groan, one sigh, one circumstance of misery, it can never be imagined that ever he should, after this, deny or withhold from his people, for whose sakes all this was suffered, any mercies, any comforts, any privilege, spiritual or temporal, which is good for them.[49]

When I first read this, I copied it into my journal and added a prayer. It is still my prayer for myself and for you, the reader.

Oh, Lord, I believe, help my wretched unbelief. What a life! Free from murmuring and complaint, and full of risk and joy and love! O, to believe this! God, I want to live in this reality. Help me. O, spare me nothing that would put me in this glorious confidence.

And now I add, Teach me how to battle the opposite, O Lord. Make me an unrelenting enemy of all unbelief in my own heart. Show me more warrior skills for how to wield the sword of the Spirit to slay the dragons of deceit and doubt in my own soul. If there is a way to live more fully by faith in this invincible future grace, I want to know that life. O Lord, let us lay hold on the logic of heaven and break out into the freedom of love and risk and suffering and death for the glory of Christ and the good of all people. That's one of the main reasons I have written this book—if by any means I might come into the deeper experience of living by faith in future grace, and take as many people with me as I can. I pray that you will come with me.

# NOTES

1. Ernest Gordon, *To End All Wars* (Grand Rapids, Michigan: Zondervan, 1963), pp. 101–102.

2. John Piper, *The Purifying Power of Living by Faith in Future Grace* (Sisters, Oregon: Multnomah Publishers, 1995).

3. This is the crucial point that I try to develop more fully in John Piper, *God Is the Gospel: Meditations on God's Love as the Gift of Himself* (Wheaton, Illinois: Crossway Books, 2005).

4. John Owen, *Mortification of Sin,* in *The Works of John Owen*, Vol. 6, edited by William H. Goold (Edinburgh: The Banner of Truth, 1967), p. 9.

5. For an explanation of what "all things" means, see *Future Grace,* chapter 8.

6. Ralph Georgy, "If God Is Dead, Then the Late 20th Century Buried Him," Minneapolis *Star Tribune,* September 12, 1994.

7. Quoted from Stephen Charnock, in *A Puritan Golden Treasury* (Edinburgh: The Banner of Truth, 1977), p. 223.

8. John Piper, *Future Grace*, chapters 14, 15, 16.

9. G. K. Chesterton, *Orthodoxy* (Garden City, New York: Image Books, Doubleday and Company, 1959, orig. 1924), p. 31.

10. A quote from *Mere Christianity* cited in *A Mind Awake: An Anthology of C. S. Lewis,* Clyde Kilby, ed., (New York: Harcourt, Brace and World, Inc., 1968), p. 115.

11. C. S. Lewis, *Letters of C. S. Lewis,* ed., W. H. Lewis, (New York: Harcourt, Brace and World, Inc., 1966), p. 256.

12. John Piper, *Desiring God: Meditations of a Christian Hedonist* (Portland, Oregon: Multnomah, 1986, 1996, 2003), p. 302.

13. Christian Hedonism is a vision of God and of life that attempts to live in light of the biblical truth that God is most glorified in us when we are most satisfied in him. It aims to glorify God by enjoying him above all things. And it fights sin by cultivating a superior satisfaction in God. The fullest statement I have given of

it is found in John Piper, *Desiring God*. Another effort to unfold the roots of Christian Hedonism is also found in John Piper, *God's Passion for His Glory: Living the Vision of Jonathan Edwards* (Wheaton, Illinois: Crossway, 1998).

14. I am aware that in common psychological parlance this has not been the definition. The common definition in psychotherapy has been this: "While guilt is a painful feeling of regret and responsibility for one's actions, shame is a painful feeling about oneself as a person." Quoted from *Facing Shame* by M. Fossum and M. Mason, in John Bradshaw, *Healing the Shame That Binds You*, (Deerfield Beach, Florida: Health Communications, Inc., 1988), p. 17. I do not embrace this definition, first, because it is not the definition used in Scripture. So the use of it makes understanding and applying Scripture more difficult. Secondly, I don't use it because it generally goes hand in hand with an assessment of the human situation that minimizes the biblical doctrine of original sin (Bradshaw, p. 65), relativizes moral absolutes (Bradshaw, p. 199), rejects biblical conditions of love (Bradshaw, p. 120), and turns God into the spiritual embodiment of absolutely unconditional approval, which never says, "should," "ought," or "must."

15. Sometimes we speak of all our sins, past, present and future, as already forgiven in the past, since they were "condemned" in the death of Jesus (Romans 8:3) and covered by the blood of Christ (Hebrews 9:14; 10:12) and forgiven through his blood (Ephesians 1:7). Other times we speak of God forgiving us in an ongoing way as we confess our sins (John 1:9) and ask for forgiveness (Matthew 6:12) on the basis of the once-for-all atonement that he made for us in Christ.

16. Karl Olsson, *Passion* (New York: Harper and Row Publishers, 1963), pp. 116–117.

17. See *Future Grace*, chapter 17.

18. Richard Wurmbrand, *One Hundred Prison Meditations* (Middlebury, Indiana: Living Sacrifice Books, 1982), pp. 6–7.

19. See Roger Nicole, "B. B. Warfield and the Calvinist Revival," in John D. Woodbridge, ed., *Great Leaders of the Christian Church* (Chicago: Moody Press, 1988), p. 344.

20. B. B. Warfield, *Faith and Life* (Edinburgh: The Banner of Truth,

1974, orig. 1914), p. 204.

21. See *Future Grace*, chapter 29.

22. H. C. G. Moule, *Charles Simeon* (London: The InterVarsity Fellowship, 1948, orig. 1892), p. 39.

23. Ibid., p. 172.

24. Martin Luther, *Freedom of a Christian,* in *Three Treatises* (Philadelphia: Fortress Press, 1960), p. 284.

25. See *Future Grace*, chapter 16.

26. Jonathan Edwards, "The End of the Wicked Contemplated by the Righteous," in *The Works of Jonathan Edwards,* Vol. 2, (Edinburgh: Banner of Truth, 1974), pp. 207–208. Edwards explains further "why the sufferings of the wicked will not cause grief to the righteous, but the contrary." He says,

> *Negatively;* it will not be because the saints in heaven are the subjects of any ill disposition; but on the contrary, this rejoicing of theirs will be the fruit of an amiable and excellent disposition: it will be the fruit of a perfect holiness and conformity to Christ, the holy Lamb of God. The devil delights in the misery of men from cruelty, and from envy and revenge, and because he delights in misery, for its own sake, from a malicious disposition.
>
> But it will be from exceedingly different principles, and for quite other reasons, that the just damnation of the wicked will be an occasion of rejoicing to the saints in glory. It will not be because they delight in seeing the misery of others absolutely considered. The damned, suffering divine vengeance, will be no occasion of joy to the saints merely as it is the misery of others, or because it is pleasant to them to behold the misery of others merely for its own sake.... It is not to be understood, that they are to rejoice in having their revenge glutted, but to rejoice in seeing the justice of God executed, and in seeing his love to them in executing it on his enemies.
>
> *Positively;* the sufferings of the damned will be no occasion of grief to the heavenly inhabitants, as they will have *no love nor pity* to the damned as such. It will be no argument of want of a spirit of love in them, that they do not love the damned; for the heavenly inhabitants will know that it is not fit that they should love them, because they will know then, that God has no love to them, nor pity for them."

Edwards raises the objection that, since it is right and good that we grieve over the faithlessness and lostness of men now in this age (Romans 9:1–3; Luke 19:41), surely it would be right to feel the same in the age to come. He answers, "It is now our duty to love all men, though they are wicked; but it will not be a duty to love wicked men hereafter. Christ, by many precepts in his word has made it our duty to love all men. We are commanded to love wicked men, and our enemies and persecutors, but this command doth not extend to the saints in glory, with respect to the damned in hell. Nor is there the same reason that it should. We ought now to love all and even wicked men; we know not but that God loves them. However wicked any man is, yet we know not but that he is one whom God loved from eternity; we know not but that Christ loved him with a dying love, had his name upon his heart before the world was, and had respect to him when he endured those bitter agonies on the cross. We know not but that he is to be our companion in glory to all eternity...."

We ought now to seek and be concerned for the salvation of wicked men, because now they are capable subjects of it.... It is yet a day of grace with them and they have the offers of salvation. Christ is as yet seeking their salvation; he is calling upon them inviting and wooing them; he stands at the door and knocks. He is using many means with them, is calling them, saying *Turn ye, turn ye, why will ye die*?... But it will not be so in another world: there wicked men will be no longer capable subjects of mercy. The saints will know, that it is the will of God the wicked should be miserable to all eternity. It will therefore cease to be their duty any more to seek their salvation, or to be concerned about their misery. On the other hand it will be their duty to rejoice in the will and glory of God. It is not our duty to be sorry that God hath executed just vengeance on the devils, concerning whom the will of God in their eternal state is already known to us (pp. 208–210).

27. Edwards, "The End of the Wicked Contemplated by the Righteous," p. 210.

28. Edward John Carnell, *Christian Commitment* (New York: Macmillan Company, 1957), pp. 94–95.

29. Thomas Watson, *Body of Divinity* (Grand Rapids, Michigan: Baker Book House, 1979, orig. 1692), p. 581. Watson's definition of

forgiveness is very helpful, both for what it says and what it does not say. He asks, "When do we forgive others?" And he answers, "When we strive against all thoughts of revenge; when we will not do our enemies mischief, but wish well to them, grieve at their calamities, pray for them, seek reconciliation with them and show ourselves ready on all occasions to relieve them" (p. 581).

30. The ESV reads "entrusting himself to him who judges justly." But the word "himself" is not in the original Greek. It simply says "entrusting to him who judges justly."

31. I deal more directly with the more complicated issues of depression and unremitting darkness in *When I Don't Desire God: How to Fight for Joy* (Wheaton, Illinois: Crossway, 2004), chapter 12, "When the Darkness Does Not Lift." See also the small book from Crossway based on this chapter, titled "When the Darkness Does not Lift."

32. Martyn Lloyd-Jones, *Spiritual Depression* (Grand Rapids: Eerdmans, 1965). p 37.

33. Ibid., p. 6.

34. Ibid., p. 109.

35. Edwards, *The Life of David Brainerd,* ed. Norman Pettit, in *The Works of Jonathan Edwards,* Vol. 7, (New Haven: Yale University Press, 1985), p. 64.

36. Ibid., p. 101.

37. Ibid., pp. 93, 141, 165, 278.

38. Lloyd-Jones, *Spiritual Depression,* pp. 18-19.

39. Darrel W. Amundsen, "The Anguish and Agonies of Charles Spurgeon" in *Christian History,* Issue 29 (Vol. 10, No. 1), p. 24.

40. Charles Spurgeon, *Lectures to My Students* (Grand Rapids, Michigan: Zondervan, 1972), p. 163.

41. Amundsen, "The Anguish and Agonies of Charles Spurgeon," p. 24.

42. Lloyd-Jones, *Spiritual Depression,* p. 20; italics added.

43. Ibid., pp. 20–21.

44. Reported in the Minneapolis *Star Tribune,* July 22, 1993.

45. This quote comes from Dabney's compelling essay on the necessity of good works (including sexual purity) in the light of free justification by grace through faith, Robert L. Dabney, "The Moral Effects of Free Justification," in *Discussions: Evangelical and Theological* (London: The Banner of Truth, 1967, orig. 1890), p. 96.

46. See *Future Grace*, chapters 18–20.
47. "The Anatomy of Lust," *Leadership* (Fall 1982), pp. 43–44.
48. See "The Debtor's Ethic: Should We Try to Pay God Back?" and "When Gratitude Malfunctions" in John Piper, *The Purifying Power of Living by Faith in Future Grace* (Sisters, Oregon: Multnomah, 1995), pp. 31–64.
49. John Flavel, *The Works of John Flavel* (Edinburgh: Banner of Truth, reprint, 1988), p. 418.

# Sever the Root of Sin

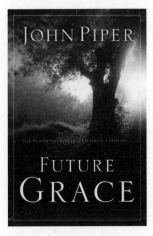

ISBN: 1-59052-191-9

THIS BOOK HELPS YOU discover the key to overcoming sin and living a life that honors God. John Piper encourages you to look ahead to the grace God provides for you on a day-by-day, moment-by-moment basis.

# Listen and Tremble

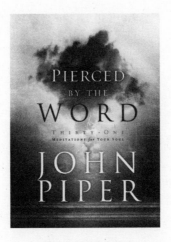

ISBN:1-59052-173-0

EXPERIENCE THE POWER of God's Word in every aspect of your life with this devotional from John Piper, author of *Desiring God*.

# Life Is Short.
# Eternity Is Long.
# Live Like It.

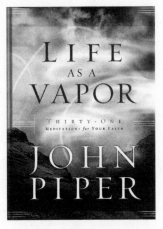

ISBN: 1-59052-338-5

HOLD ON TO WHAT will stand. Savor what matters. This collection of thirty-one articles is full of that heart-longing after Christ that distinguishes Piper's preaching ministry.

# Be Satisfied in God
# Because God
# Is Satisfied in God.

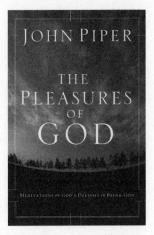

ISBN: 1-57673-665-2

IN THIS RERELEASE OF a classic, you will find satisfaction in God by knowing why God himself is most satisfied in God. Essential, life-changing truths are presented in a delightful, easy-to-grasp manner.